Getting Started
with Ubuntu 12.10

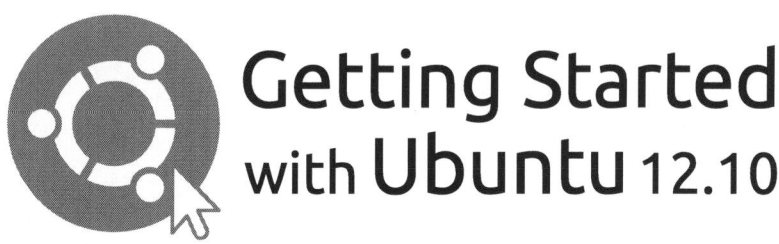

The Ubuntu Manual Team

Copyright © 2010–2012 by The Ubuntu Manual Team. Some rights reserved.
©⊕⊚

This work is licensed under the Creative Commons Attribution–Share Alike 3.0 License. To view a copy of this license, see Appendix A, visit http://creativecommons.org/licenses/by-sa/3.0/, or send a letter to Creative Commons, 171 Second Street, Suite 300, San Francisco, California, 94105, USA.

Getting Started with Ubuntu 12.10 can be downloaded for free from http://ubuntu-manual.org/ or purchased from http://ubuntu-manual.org/buy/gswu1210/en_US. A printed copy of this book can be ordered for the price of printing and delivery. We permit and even encourage you to distribute a copy of this book to colleagues, friends, family, and anyone else who might be interested.

http://ubuntu-manual.org

Revision number: 179   Revision date: 2012-12-14 12:58:35 -0600

Contents

    Prologue 5
        Welcome 5
        Ubuntu Philosophy 5
        A brief history of Ubuntu 6
        Is Ubuntu right for you? 7
        Contact details 8
        About the team 8
        Conventions used in this book 8

1   Installation 9
        Getting Ubuntu 9
        Trying out Ubuntu 10
        Installing Ubuntu—Getting started 11
        Finishing Installation 17
        Ubuntu installer for Windows 18

2   The Ubuntu Desktop 21
        Understanding the Ubuntu desktop 21
        Unity 21
        Using the Launcher 23
        The Dash 24
        Workspaces 26
        Managing windows 26
        Browsing files on your computer 28
        Nautilus file manager 28
        Searching for files and folders on your computer 30
        Customizing your desktop 31
        Accessibility 32
        Session options 33
        Getting help 34

3   Working with Ubuntu 37
        All the applications you need 37
        Getting online 39
        Browsing the web 46
        Reading and composing email 55
        Using instant messaging 59
        Microblogging 63
        Viewing and editing photos 66
        Watching videos and movies 69
        Listening to audio and music 70
        Burning CDs and DVDs 75
        Working with documents, spreadsheets, and presentations 78
        Ubuntu One 78

4   Hardware 89
        Using your devices 89
        Hardware identification 89

Displays 89
Connecting and using your printer 91
Sound 92
Using a webcam 93
Scanning text and images 93
Other devices 94

5 Software Management 97
Software management in Ubuntu 97
Using the Ubuntu Software Center 97
Managing additional software 101
Manual software installation 104
Updates and upgrades 105

6 Advanced Topics 107
Ubuntu for advanced users 107
Introduction to the terminal 107
Ubuntu file system structure 108
Securing Ubuntu 110
Why Ubuntu is safe 110
Basic security concepts 110
User accounts 111
System updates 113
Firewall 113
Encryption 114

7 Troubleshooting 115
Resolving problems 115
Troubleshooting guide 115
Getting more help 120

8 Learning More 121
What else can I do with Ubuntu? 121
Open source software 121
Distribution families 121
Choosing amongst Ubuntu and its derivatives 122
Finding additional help and support 123
The Ubuntu community 125
Contributing 126

A License 127
Creative Commons Attribution–ShareAlike 3.0 Legal Code 127
Creative Commons Notice 133

Glossary 135

Credits 137

Index 139

Prologue

Welcome

Welcome to *Getting Started with Ubuntu*, an introductory guide written to help new users get started with Ubuntu.

Our goal is to cover the basics of Ubuntu (such as installation and working with the desktop) as well as hardware and software management, working with the command line, and security. We designed this guide to be simple to follow, with step-by-step instructions and plenty of screenshots, allowing you to discover the potential of your new Ubuntu system.

Ubuntu 12.10 is considered a regular release and is supported by Canonical with patches and upgrades for eighteen months. Ubuntu 12.04 is the most recent LTS and has support for 5 years. Whenever a new version of Ubuntu is released, we will incorporate updates and changes into our guide, and make a new version available at http://www.ubuntu-manual.org.

Getting Started with Ubuntu 12.10 is not intended to be a comprehensive Ubuntu instruction manual. It is more like a quick-start guide that will get you doing the things you need to do with your computer quickly and easily, without getting bogged down with technical details. As with prior versions, Ubuntu 12.10 incorporates many new features, including a new kernel supporting newer graphics cards, updates to the Update Manager, and full-disk encryption, to name just a few.

For more detailed information on any aspect of the Ubuntu desktop, see the "Ubuntu Desktop Guide," which can be obtained in any of the following ways:

- in the Dash, type **help**.
- in the desktop menu bar, click **Help ▸ Ubuntu Help**.
- go to https://help.ubuntu.com, **Ubuntu 12.10 ▸ Ubuntu Desktop Help**.

There are also many excellent resources available on the Internet. For example, on https://help.ubuntu.com you will find documentation on installing and using Ubuntu. At the Ubuntu Forums (http://ubuntuforums.org) and Ask Ubuntu (http://askubuntu.com), you will find answers to many Ubuntu-related questions.

If something isn't covered in this manual, chances are you will find the information you are looking for in one of those locations. We will try our best to include links to more detailed help wherever we can.

> You can find more information about Ubuntu's online and system documentation in Chapter 8: Learning More.

Ubuntu Philosophy

The term "Ubuntu" is a traditional African concept originating from the Bantu languages of southern Africa. It can be described as a way of connecting with others—living in a global community where your actions affect all of humanity. Ubuntu is more than just an operating system: it is a community of people coming together voluntarily to collaborate on an international software project that aims to deliver the best possible user experience.

> People sometimes wonder how to pronounce *Ubuntu*. Each *u* is pronounced the same as in the word *put* except for the last *u* which is pronounced the same as in the word *due*.

The Ubuntu Promise

- Ubuntu will always be free of charge, along with its regular enterprise releases and security updates.
- Ubuntu comes with full commercial support from Canonical and hundreds of companies from across the world.
- Ubuntu provides the best translations and accessibility features that the free software community has to offer.
- Ubuntu's core applications are all free and open source. We want you to use free and open source software, improve it, and pass it on.

A brief history of Ubuntu

Ubuntu was conceived in 2004 by Mark Shuttleworth, a successful South African entrepreneur, and his company Canonical. Shuttleworth recognized the power of Linux and open source, but was also aware of weaknesses that prevented mainstream use.

Shuttleworth set out with clear intentions to address these weaknesses and create a system that was easy to use, completely free (see Chapter 8: Learning More for the complete definition of "free"), and could compete with other mainstream operating systems. With the Debian system as a base, Shuttleworth began to build Ubuntu. Using his own funds at first, installation CDs were pressed and shipped worldwide at no cost to the recipients. Ubuntu spread quickly, its community grew rapidly, and soon Ubuntu became the most popular Linux distribution available.

Canonical is the company that provides financial and technical support for Ubuntu. It has employees based around the world who work on developing and improving the operating system, as well as reviewing work submitted by volunteer contributors. To learn more about Canonical, go to http://www.canonical.com.

Debian is the Linux operating system that Ubuntu is based upon. For more information visit http://www.debian.org/.

With more people working on the project than ever before, its core features and hardware support continue to improve, and Ubuntu has gained the attention of large organizations worldwide. One of IBM's open source operating systems is based on Ubuntu. In 2005, the French Police began to transition their entire computer infrastructure to a variant of Ubuntu—a process which has reportedly saved them "millions of euros" in licensing fees for Microsoft Windows. By the end of 2012, the French Police anticipates that all of their computers will be running Ubuntu. Canonical profits from this arrangement by providing technical support and custom-built software.

While large organizations often find it useful to pay for support services, Shuttleworth has promised that the Ubuntu desktop operating system will always be free. As of 2012, Ubuntu is installed on an estimated 2% of the world's computers. This equates to tens of millions of users worldwide, and is growing each year. As there is no compulsory registration, the percentage of Ubuntu users should be treated as an estimate.

For information on Ubuntu Server Edition, and how you can use it in your company, visit http://www.ubuntu.com/business/server/overview.

What is Linux?

Ubuntu is built on the foundation of Linux, which is a member of the Unix family. Unix is one of the oldest types of operating systems, and together with Linux has provided reliability and security for professional applications for almost half a century. Many servers around the world that store data for popular websites (such as YouTube and Google) run some variant of Linux or Unix. The popular Android system for smartphones is a Linux variant; modern in-car computers usually run on Linux. Even the Mac OS X is based on Unix. The Linux kernel is best described as the core—almost the brain—of the Ubuntu operating system.

The Linux kernel is the controller of the operating system; it is responsible for allocating memory and processor time. It can also be thought of as the program which manages any and all applications on the computer itself.

Linux was designed from the ground up with security and hardware compatibility in mind, and is currently one of the most popular Unix-based operating systems. One of the benefits of Linux is that it is incredibly flexible and can be configured to run on almost any device—from the smallest micro-computers and cellphones to the largest super-computers. Unix was entirely command line-based until graphical user interfaces (GUIs) emerged in 1973 (in comparison, Apple came out with Mac OS ten years later, and Microsoft released Windows 1.0 in 1985).

The early GUIs were difficult to configure, clunky, and generally only used by seasoned computer programmers. In the past decade, however, graphical user interfaces have grown in usability, reliability, and appearance. Ubuntu is just one of many different Linux *distributions*, and uses one of the more popular graphical desktop environments called GNOME.

> While modern graphical desktop environments have generally replaced early command-line interfaces, the command line can still be a quick and efficient way of performing many tasks. See Chapter 6: Advanced Topics for more information, and Chapter 2: The Ubuntu Desktop to learn more about GNOME and other desktop environments.

> To learn more about Linux distributions, see Chapter 8: Learning More.

Is Ubuntu right for you?

New users to Ubuntu may find that it takes some time to feel comfortable when trying a new operating system. You will no doubt notice many similarities to both Microsoft Windows and Mac OS X as well as some differences. Users coming from Mac OS X are more likely to notice similarities due to the fact that both Mac OS X and Ubuntu originated from Unix. The Unity shell, which is the default in Ubuntu, is a completely new concept, which needs some exploring to get used to it. See Chapter 2: The Ubuntu Desktop for more information about the Unity shell.

Before you decide whether or not Ubuntu is right for you, we suggest giving yourself some time to grow accustomed to the way things are done in Ubuntu. You should expect to find that some things are different from what you are used to. We also suggest taking the following into account:

Ubuntu is community based. That is, Ubuntu is developed, written, and maintained by the community. Because of this, support is probably not available at your local computer store. Fortunately, the Ubuntu community is here to help. There are many articles, guides, and manuals available, as well as users on various Internet forums and Internet Relay Chat (IRC) rooms that are willing to assist beginners. Additionally, near the end of this guide, we include a troubleshooting chapter: Chapter 7: Troubleshooting.

Many applications designed for Microsoft Windows or Mac OS X will not run on Ubuntu. For the vast majority of everyday computing tasks, you will find suitable alternative applications available in Ubuntu. However, many professional applications (such as the Adobe Creative Suite) are not developed to work with Ubuntu. If you rely on commercial software that is not compatible with Ubuntu, yet still want to give Ubuntu a try, you may want to consider dual-booting. Alternatively, some applications developed for Windows will work in Ubuntu with a program called Wine. For more information on Wine, go to http://www.winehq.org.

Many commercial games will not run on Ubuntu. If you are a heavy gamer, then Ubuntu may not be for you. Game developers usually design games for the largest market. Since Ubuntu's market share is not as substantial as Microsoft's Windows or Apple's Mac OS X, fewer game developers allocate resources towards making their games compatible with Linux. If

> To learn more about dual-booting (running Ubuntu side-by-side with another operating system), see Chapter 1: Installation.

> See Chapter 5: Software Management to learn more about Ubuntu Software Center.

you just enjoy a game every now and then, there are many high quality games that can be easily installed through the Ubuntu Software Center.

Contact details

Many people have contributed their time to this project. If you notice any errors or think we have left something out, feel free to contact us. We do everything we can to make sure that this manual is up to date, informative, and professional. Our contact details are as follows:

- Website: http://www.ubuntu-manual.org/
- Reader feedback: feedback@ubuntu-manual.org
- IRC: #ubuntu-manual on irc.freenode.net
- Bug Reports: https://bugs.launchpad.net/ubuntu-manual/+filebug
- Mailing list: ubuntu-manual@lists.launchpad.net

About the team

Our project is an open-source, volunteer effort to create and maintain quality documentation for Ubuntu and its derivatives.

Want to help?

We are always looking for talented people to work with, and due to the size of the project we are fortunate to be able to cater to a wide range of skill sets:

- Authors and editors
- Programmers (Python or TeX)
- User interface designers
- Icon and title page designers
- Event organizers and ideas people
- Testers
- Web designers and developers
- Translators and screenshotters
- Bug reporters and triagers

To find out how you can get started helping, please visit http://ubuntu-manual.org/getinvolved.

Conventions used in this book

The following typographic conventions are used in this book:

- Button names, menu items, and other GUI elements are set in **boldfaced type**.
- Menu sequences are sometimes typeset as **File ▸ Save As...**, which means, "Choose the **File** menu, then choose the **Save As...**."
- `Monospaced` type is used for text that you type into the computer, text that the computer outputs (as in a terminal), and keyboard shortcuts.

1 Installation

Getting Ubuntu

Before you can get started with Ubuntu, you will need to obtain a copy of the Ubuntu installation image for DVD or USB. Some options for doing this are outlined below.

Many companies (such as Dell and System76) sell computers with Ubuntu preinstalled. If you already have Ubuntu installed on your computer, feel free to skip to Chapter 2: The Ubuntu Desktop.

Minimum system requirements

Ubuntu runs well on most computer systems. If you are unsure whether it will work on your computer, the Live DVD is a great way to test things out first. Below is a list of hardware specifications that your computer should meet as a minimum requirement.

The majority of computers in use today will meet the requirements listed here; however, refer to your computer documentation or manufacturer's website for more information.

- 1 GHz x86 processor (Pentium 4 or better)
- 1 GB of system memory (RAM)
- 5 GB of disk space (at least 15 GB is recommended)
- Video support capable of 1024×768 resolution
- Audio support
- An Internet connection (highly recommended, but not required)

Downloading Ubuntu

The easiest and most common method for getting Ubuntu is to download the Ubuntu DVD image directly from http://www.ubuntu.com/download. Choose how you will install Ubuntu:

- Download and install
- Try it from a DVD or USB stick
- Run it with Windows

Download and Install / Try it from a DVD or USB stick

For the *Download and install*, or *Try it from a DVD or USB stick* options, select whether you require the 32-bit or 64-bit version (32-bit is recommended for most users), then click "Start download."

Installing and run alongside Windows

For the *Run it with Windows* option, simply select "Start download," and then follow the instructions for the Ubuntu installer for Windows.

32-bit versus 64-bit

Ubuntu and its derivatives are available in two versions: 32-bit and 64-bit. This difference refers to the way computers process information. Computers capable of running 64-bit software are able to process more information than computers running 32-bit software; however, 64-bit systems require more memory in order to do this. Nevertheless, these computers gain performance enhancements by running 64-bit software.

32-bit and 64-bit are types of processor architectures. Most new desktop computers have a 64-bit capable processor.

- If your computer has a 64-bit processor install the 64-bit version.

- If your computer is older, a netbook, or you do not know the type of processor in the computer, install the 32-bit version.

If your computer has a 64-bit processor, click on the "64-bit" option before you click "Start download."

Downloading Ubuntu as a torrent

When a new version of Ubuntu is released, the download servers can get "clogged" as large numbers of people try to download or upgrade Ubuntu at the same time. If you are familiar with using torrents, you can download the torrent file by clicking "Alternative downloads," and then "BitTorrent download." Downloading via torrent may improve your download speed, and will also be help to spread Ubuntu to other users worldwide.

Torrents are a way of sharing files and information around the Internet via peer-to-peer file sharing. A file with the .torrent extension is made available to users, which is then opened with a compatible program such as uTorrent, Deluge, or Transmission. These programs download parts of the file from other people all around the world.

Burning the DVD image

Once your download is complete, you will be left with a file called *ubuntu-12.10-desktop-i386.iso* or similar (*i386* here in the filename refers to the 32-bit version. If you downloaded the 64-bit version, the filename contains *amd64* instead). This file is a DVD image—a snapshot of the contents of a DVD—which you will need to burn to a DVD.

While the 64-bit version of Ubuntu is referred to as the "AMD64" version, it will work on Intel, AMD, and other compatible 64-bit processors.

Creating a bootable USB drive

If your PC is able to boot from a USB stick, you may prefer to use a USB memory stick instead of burning a DVD. Scroll down to "Burn your DVD or create a USB drive," select DVD or *USB stick*, choose the OS you are using to create the USB drive, and then click *Show me how*. If you select the "USB Stick" option, your installation will be running from the USB memory stick. In this case, references to Live DVD, will refer to the USB memory stick.

Trying out Ubuntu

The Ubuntu DVD and USB stick function not only as installation media, but also allow you to test Ubuntu without making any permanent changes to your computer by running the entire operating system from the DVD or USB stick.

Your computer reads information from a DVD at a much slower speed than it can read information off of a hard drive. Running Ubuntu from the Live DVD also occupies a large portion of your computer's memory, which would usually be available for applications to access when Ubuntu is running from your hard drive. The Live DVD/USB experience will therefore feel slightly slower than it does when Ubuntu is actually installed on your computer. Running Ubuntu from the DVD/USB is a great way to test things out and allows you to try the default applications, browse the Internet, and get a general feel for the operating system. It's also useful for checking that your computer hardware works properly in Ubuntu and that there are no major compatibility issues.

To try out Ubuntu using the Live DVD/USB stick, insert the Ubuntu DVD into your DVD drive, or connect the USB drive and restart your computer.

After your computer finds the Live DVD/USB stick, and a quick loading screen, you will be presented with the "Welcome" screen. Using your mouse, select your language from the list on the left, then click the button

In some cases, your computer will not recognize that the Ubuntu DVD or USB is present as it starts up and will start your existing operating system instead. Generally, this means that the priority given to *boot devices* when your computer is starting needs to be changed. For example, your computer might be set to look for information from your hard drive, and then to look for information on a DVD or USB. To run Ubuntu from the Live DVD or USB, we want the computer to look for information from the appropriate device first. Changing your *boot priority* is usually handled by BIOS settings; this is beyond the scope of this guide. If you need assistance with changing the boot priority, see your computer manufacturer's documentation for more information.

labeled **Try Ubuntu**. Ubuntu will then start up, running directly from the Live DVD/USB drive.

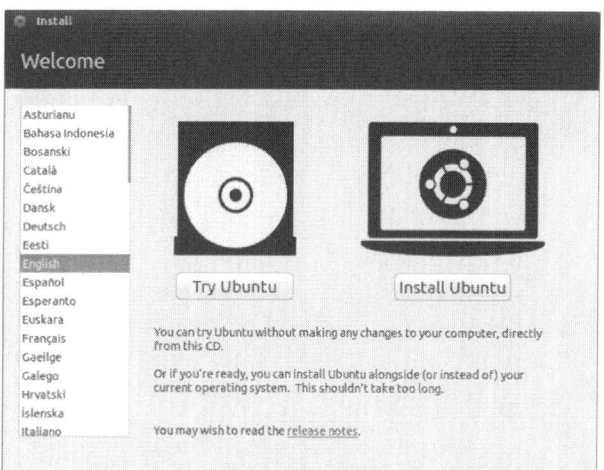

Figure 1.1: The "Welcome" screen allows you to choose your language.

Once Ubuntu is up and running, you will see the default desktop. We will talk more about how to actually use Ubuntu in Chapter 2: The Ubuntu Desktop, but for now, feel free to test things out. Open some applications, change settings and generally explore—any changes you make will not be saved once you exit, so you don't need to worry about accidentally breaking anything.

When you are finished exploring, restart your computer by clicking the "Power" button in the top right corner of your screen (a circle with a line through the top) and then select **Restart**. Follow the prompts that appear on screen, including removing the Live DVD and pressing Enter when instructed, and then your computer will restart. As long as the Live DVD is no longer in the drive, your computer will return to its original state as though nothing ever happened!

Alternatively, you can also use your mouse to double-click the "Install Ubuntu 12.10" icon that is visible on the desktop when using the Live DVD. This will start the Ubuntu installer.

Installing Ubuntu—Getting started

At least 5 GB of free space on your hard drive is required in order to install Ubuntu; however, 15 GB or more is recommended. This will ensure that you will have plenty of room to install extra applications later on, as well as store your own documents, music, and photos. To get started, place the Ubuntu DVD in your DVD drive and restart your computer. Your computer should load Ubuntu from the DVD. When you first start from the DVD, you will be presented with a screen asking you whether you want to first try out Ubuntu or install it. Select the language you want to view the installer in and click on the **Install Ubuntu** button. This will start the installation process.

If you have an Internet connection, the installer will ask you if you would like to "Download updates while installing." We recommend you do so. The second option, "Install this third-party software," includes the Fluendo MP3 codec, and software required for some wireless hardware. If you are not connected to the Internet, the installer will help you set up a wireless connection.

The "Preparing to install Ubuntu" screen will also let you know if you have enough disk space and if you are connected to a power source (in case

Clicking on the underlined "release notes" link will open a web page containing any important information regarding the current version of Ubuntu.

you are installing Ubuntu on a laptop running on battery). Once you have selected your choices, click **Continue**.

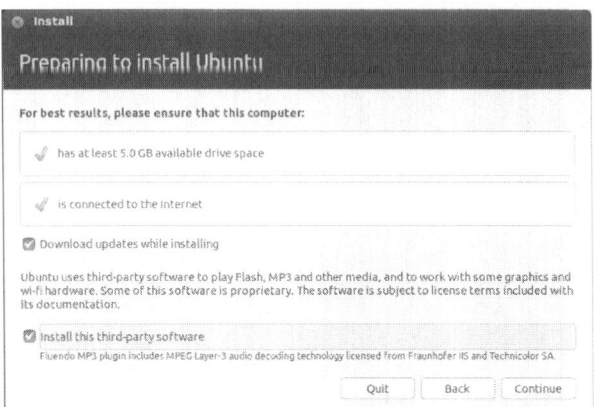

Figure 1.2: Preparing to install.

Internet connection

If you are not connected to the Internet, the installer will ask you to choose a wireless network (if available).

1. Select **Connect to this network**, and then select your network from the list.
2. If the list does not appear immediately, wait until a triangle/arrow appears next to the network adapter, and then click the arrow to see the available networks.
3. In the **Password** field, enter the network WEP or WPA key (if necessary).
4. Click **Connect** to continue.

We recommend that you connect during install, though updates and third-party software can be installed after installation.

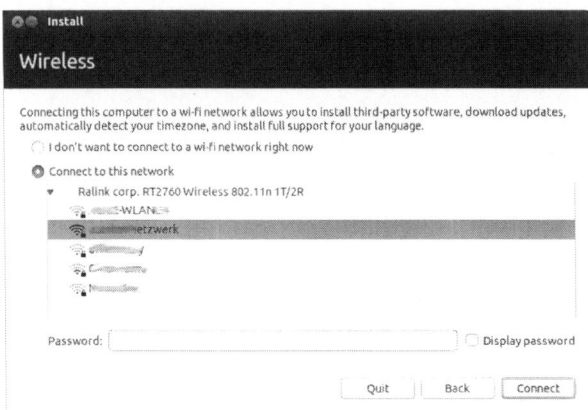

Figure 1.3: Set up wireless.

Allocate drive space

This next step is often referred to as partitioning. Partitioning is the process of allocating portions of your hard drive for a specific purpose. When you create a partition, you are essentially dividing up your hard drive into sections that will be used for different types of information. Partitioning can sometimes seem complex to a new user; however, it does not have to be. In

If you are installing on a new machine with no operating system, you will not get the first option. The upgrade option is only available if you are upgrading from a previous version of Ubuntu.

fact, Ubuntu provides you with some options that greatly simplify this process. The Ubuntu installer will automatically detect any existing operating system installed on your machine, and present installation options suitable for your system. The options listed below depend on your specific system and may not all be available:

- Install alongside other operating systems
- Install inside Windows
- Upgrade Ubuntu ... to 12.10
- Erase ... and install Ubuntu
- Something else

Install alongside other operating systems.

If you are a Windows or Mac user and you are trying to install Ubuntu for the first time, select the **Install alongside other operating systems** option. This option will enable you to choose which operating system you wish to use when you computer starts. Ubuntu will automatically detect the other operating system and install Ubuntu alongside it.

Ubuntu provides you with the option of either *replacing* your existing operating system altogether, or installing Ubuntu alongside your existing system. The latter is called *dual-booting*. Whenever you turn on or restart your computer, you will be given the option to select which operating system you want to use for that session.

 For more complicated dual-booting setups, you will need to configure the partitions manually.

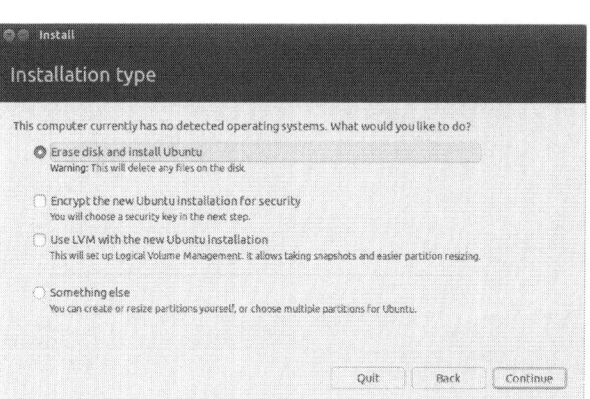

Figure 1.4: Choose where you would like to install Ubuntu.

Upgrade Ubuntu ... to 12.10

This option will keep all of your Documents, music, pictures, and other personal files. Installed software will be kept when possible (not all your currently installed software may be supported on the new version). System-wide settings will be cleared.

Erase disk and install Ubuntu

Use this option if you want to erase your entire disk. This will delete any existing operating systems that are installed on that disk, such as Microsoft Windows, and install Ubuntu in its place. This option is also useful if you have an empty hard drive, as Ubuntu will automatically create the necessary partitions for you.

 Formatting a partition will destroy any data currently on the partition. Be sure to back up any data you want to save before formatting.

Something else

This option is for advanced users and is used to create special partitions, or format the hard drive with a file system different to the default one.

After you have chosen the installation type, click **Continue**, or **Install Now**.

Confirm Partition choices and start install

If you chose **Something else**, configure the partitions as you need. Once you are happy with the way the partitions are going to be set up, click the **Install Now** button at the bottom right to move on.

To reduce the time required for installation, Ubuntu will continue the installation process in the background while you configure important user details—like your username, password, keyboard settings and default time-zone.

Where are you?

Ubuntu installs a *home folder* where your personal files and configuration data are located by default. If you choose to have your home folder on a separate partition, then in the event that you decide to reinstall Ubuntu or perform a fresh upgrade to the latest release, your personal files and configuration data won't be lost.

More information and detailed instructions on partitioning are available at: https://help.ubuntu.com/community/HowtoPartition.

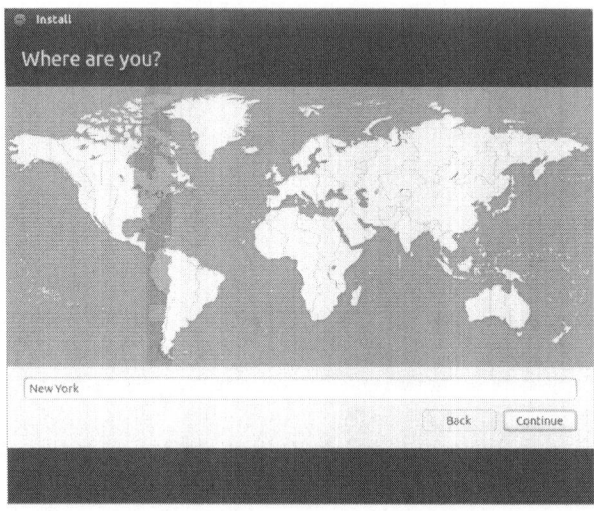

Figure 1.5: Tell Ubuntu your location.

The next screen will display a world map. Using your mouse, click your geographic location on the map to tell Ubuntu where you are. Alternatively, you can use the drop-down lists below the map. This allows Ubuntu to configure your system clock and other location-based features. Click **Forward** when you are ready to move on.

Keyboard layout

Next, you need to tell Ubuntu what kind of keyboard you are using. In most cases, you will find the suggested option satisfactory. If you are unsure which keyboard option to select, you can click the **Detect Keyboard Layout** button to have Ubuntu determine the correct choice by asking you to press a series of keys. You can also manually choose your keyboard layout from the list of options. If you like, enter text into the box at the bottom of the window to ensure you are happy with your selection, then click **Continue**.

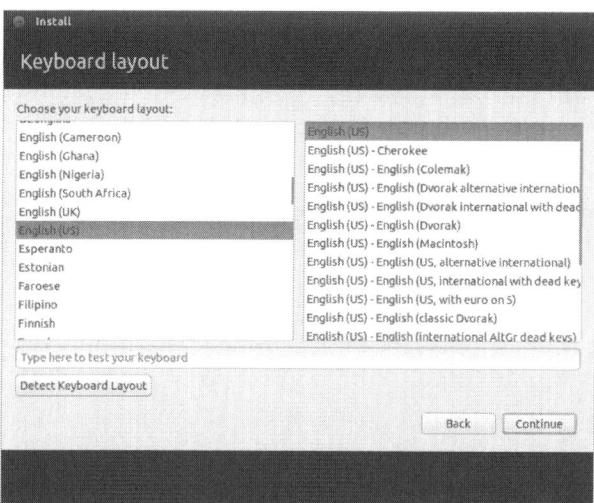

Figure 1.6: Verify that your keyboard layout is correct.

Who are you?

Ubuntu needs to know some information about you so it can set up the primary user account on your computer. When configured, your name will appear on the login screen as well as the user menu, which we discuss in Chapter 2: The Ubuntu Desktop.

On this screen you will need to tell Ubuntu:

- your name
- what you want to call your computer
- your desired username
- your desired password
- how you want Ubuntu to log you in

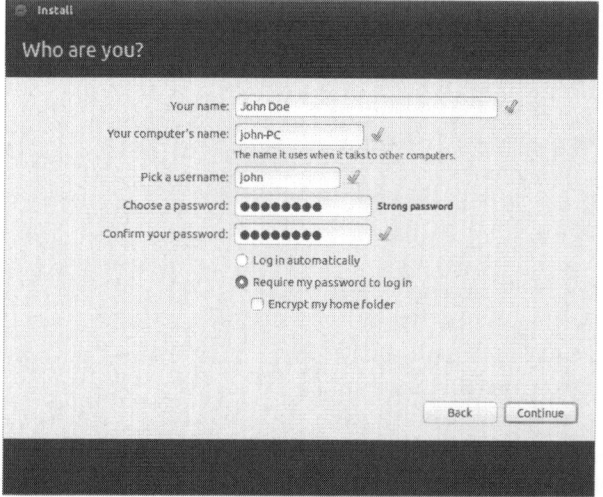

Figure 1.7: Setup your user account.

Enter your full name under **Your name**. The next text field is the name your computer uses, for terminals and networks. You can change this to what you want, or keep the predetermined name. Next is your username, the name that is used for the user menu, your home folder, and behind the scenes. You will see this is automatically filled in for you with your first name. Most people find it easiest to stick with this. However, it can be changed if you prefer.

Next, choose a password and enter it into both password fields. When both passwords match, a strength rating will appear to the right that will show you whether your password is "too short," "weak," "fair," or "strong." You will be able to continue the installation process regardless of your password strength, but for security reasons it is best to choose a strong one. This is best achieved by having a password that is at least six characters long, and is a mixture of letters, numbers, symbols, and uppercase/lowercase. Avoid obvious passwords that include your birth date, spouse's name, or the name of your pet.

Login Options

Finally, at the bottom of this screen you have three options from which to choose regarding how you wish to log in to Ubuntu.

- Log in automatically
- Require my password to log in
- Encrypt my home folder

Log in automatically

Ubuntu will log in to your primary account automatically when you start up the computer so you won't have to enter your username and password. This makes your login experience quicker and more convenient, but if privacy or security are important to you, we don't recommend this option. Anyone who can physically access your computer will be able to turn it on and also access your files.

Require my password to login

This option is selected by default, as it will prevent unauthorized people from accessing your computer without knowing the password you created earlier. This is a good option for those who, for example, share their computer with other family members. Once the installation process has been completed, an additional login account can be created for each family member. Each person will then have their own login name and password, account preferences, Internet bookmarks, and personal storage space.

Encrypt my home folder

This option provides you with an extra layer of security. Your home folder is where your personal files are stored. By selecting this option, Ubuntu will automatically enable encryption on your home folder, meaning that files and folders must be decrypted using your password before they can be accessed. Therefore if someone had physical access to your hard drive (for example, if your computer was stolen and the hard drive removed), they would not be able to see your files without knowing your password.

 If you choose this option, be careful not to enable automatic login at a later date. It will cause complications with your encrypted home folder, and will potentially lock you out of important files.

Finishing Installation

Ubuntu will now finish installing on your hard drive. As the installation progresses, a slideshow will give you an introduction to some of the default applications included with Ubuntu. These applications are covered in more detail in Chapter 3: Working with Ubuntu. The slideshow will also highlight the Ubuntu support options:

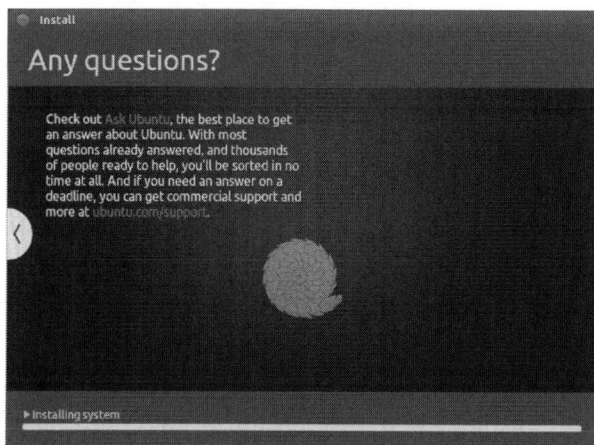

Figure 1.8: Ubuntu community support options. Where to get help for Ubuntu.

After approximately twenty minutes, the installation will complete and you will be able to click **Restart Now** to restart your computer and start Ubuntu. The DVD will be ejected, so remove it from your DVD drive and press Enter to continue.

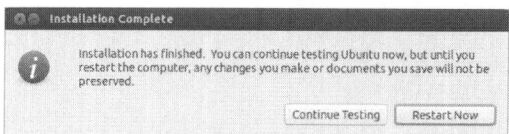

Figure 1.9: You are now ready to restart your computer.

Wait while your computer restarts, and you will then see the login window (unless you selected automatic login).

Login Screen

After the installation has finished and your computer is restarted, you will be greeted by the login screen of Ubuntu. The login screen will present you with your username and you will have to enter the password to get past it. Click your username and enter your password. Once done, you may click the arrow or press Enter to get into the Ubuntu desktop. Ubuntu's login screen supports multiple users and also supports custom backgrounds for each user. In fact, Ubuntu automatically will pick up your current desktop wallpaper and set it as your login background. Ubuntu's login screen also lets you select the different environments to login.

The login screen allows you to update your keyboard language, volume intensity and enable/disable accessibility settings before you log in to your desktop. It also displays date/time and battery power for laptops. You can also shut down or restart your system from the login screen.

A guest session is also available at the login screen. You can activate this session for guests using your laptop or desktop.

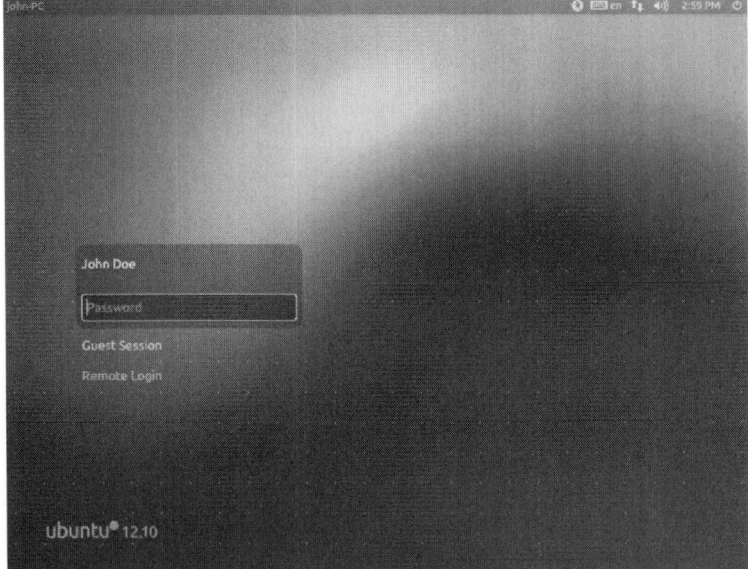

Figure 1.10: Login Screen.

Ubuntu installer for Windows

You can install and run Ubuntu alongside your current installation of Windows:

1. Download the Ubuntu installer for Windows http://www.ubuntu.com/download/ubuntu/windows-installer
2. Run the download file
3. Install Ubuntu

Download and run the installer

After the file, *wubi.exe*, is downloaded, run the file to start the installation. If a security message appears, click **Continue**, to proceed with the installation:

Installation

The Ubuntu Installer will start. Choose and enter a "Username" and "Password." The password must be entered twice to ensure accuracy. After

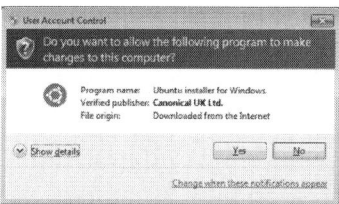

Figure 1.11: User Account Control dialog

choosing a password, click **Install**. The Ubuntu Installer will download and install Ubuntu. This process will take some time. The download file size is approximately 750 MB. After the installation is complete, click **Finish** on the "Completing the Ubuntu Setup Wizard" screen to reboot the computer.

Figure 1.12: Ubuntu Windows Installer

Installation complete

After the computer restarts, you can select "Ubuntu" from the boot menu. You will then be logged in to Ubuntu and will be presented with your new desktop!

2 The Ubuntu Desktop

Understanding the Ubuntu desktop

Initially, you may notice many similarities between Ubuntu and other operating systems, such as Microsoft Windows or Mac OS X. This is because they are all based on the concept of a graphical user interface (GUI)—*i.e.*, you use your mouse to navigate the desktop, open applications, move files, and perform most other tasks. In short, things are visually-oriented. This chapter is designed to help you become familiar with various applications and menus in Ubuntu so that you become confident in using the Ubuntu GUI.

Figure 2.1: The Ubuntu 12.10 default desktop.

Unity

All GUI-based operating systems use a *desktop environment*. Desktop environments encompass many things, such as:

- The look and feel of your system
- The way the desktop is laid out
- How the desktop is navigated by the user

In Linux distributions (such as Ubuntu), a number of desktop environments are available. Ubuntu uses Unity as the default desktop environment. After installing and logging in to Ubuntu, you will see the Unity desktop. This initial view is comprised of the desktop background and two bars—a horizontal one located at the top of your desktop called the menu bar, and the other bar is vertically oriented at the far left, called the Launcher.

To read more about other variants of Ubuntu, refer to Chapter 8: Learning More.

Unity used to come in two versions—Unity 2D, which was written for low-powered systems, and Unity 3D, which favored high-performance systems. Because of recent advancements in Unity 3D, Ubuntu 12.10 has discontinued the use of Unity 2D and now only includes Unity 3D. Unity 3D now is able to run on lower-powered systems as well as high-performance platforms.

The Desktop Background

Below the menu bar is an image that covers the entire desktop. This is the default desktop background, or wallpaper, belonging to the default Ubuntu 12.10 theme known as *Ambiance*. To learn more about customizing your desktop (including changing your background), see the section on Customizing your desktop below.

The Menu Bar

The menu bar incorporates common functions used in Ubuntu 12.10. The icons on the far-right of the menu bar are called the *indicator area*. Each installation of Ubuntu may contain slightly different types and quantities of icons based on a number of factors, including type of hardware and available on-board peripherals. The most common indicators are (starting from the left):

Keyboard indicator allows you to select the keyboard layout you would like and change your keyboard preferences.
Messaging indicator incorporates all your social applications. From here, you can access your instant messenger client, your email client, your microblogging application, and even Ubuntu One, your personal cloud!
Network indicator allows you to manage your network connections and connect quickly and easily to a wired or wireless network.
Sound indicator provides an easy way to adjust the sound volume as well as access your music player and sound settings.
Clock displays the current time and provides an easy way to access your calendar and time and date settings.
User menu allows you to easily switch between different users and access your online and user accounts.
Session indicator provides an easy way to access system settings, software updates, printers, and session options for locking your computer, logging out of your session, restarting the computer, or shutting down completely.

Every application has a menuing system where different actions can be executed in an application (like **File**, **Edit**, **View**, etc.); the menuing system for an application is appropriately called the **application menu**. In Unity, the *application menu* isn't on the titlebar of the application as is commonly the case with other GUI environments. Instead, it is located to the left area of the menu bar. To show an application's menu, just move your mouse to the Ubuntu desktop's menu bar. While your mouse is positioned here, the active application's menu options will superimpose itself over the Ubuntu desktop's menu bar, allowing you to use the application's menus. Moving your mouse away from the menu bar will allow Ubuntu desktop's menu bar to reappear. This capability of Unity to only show the application's menu when needed is especially beneficial for netbook and laptop users as it provides you with more free work space.

For more about:
- the Messaging Indicator see Microblogging;
- the Network Indicator see Getting online;
- the Session Indicator see Session options.

The *keyboard indicator* only appears when you have chosen more than one keyboard layout in the keyboard settings during installation.

Figure 2.2: The Indicators of the menu bar.

Note that some older applications may still display their menu within the application window.

The Launcher

Figure 2.3: The Ubuntu 12.10 Launcher on the left with a sample of applications on it.

The vertical bar of icons on the left side of the screen is called the Launcher. The Launcher provides easy access to applications, mounted devices, and the **Trash**. All running applications on your system will place an icon in the Launcher while the application is running. The first icon at the top of the Launcher is the Dash, a major innovation and core element of Unity—we will explore the Dash in a later section of this chapter. By default, other applications appear on the Launcher, including LibreOffice and Firefox, the **workspace switcher** lens, any mounted devices, and, of course, the always-important **Trash** lens at the bottom of the Launcher.

The workspace switcher helps you to select the workspace or the window you want. **Trash** contains deleted files.

Tip: Pressing Super+S will show the content of the workspaces on one screen. Super key is also known as the Windows key (Win key). It is located between the left Strg key and Alt key.

If you hold the Super key, a number will appear on each of the first ten applications, along with a margin containing useful shortcuts. You can launch an application with a number *n* on it by typing Super+*n*.

Using the Launcher

Running applications

To run an application from the Launcher (or cause an already-running application to appear), just click on the application's icon. Running applications will have one or more triangles on the left side of the icon, indicating the number of application windows open for this application. The application in the foreground (meaning on top of all other open application windows) is indicated by a single white triangle on the right side of its icon. You can also run an application through the Dash. We will talk about the Dash, in the The Dash section.

Figure 2.4: Just below the Home Folder icon, you will see the Firefox icon. Notice the triangle on the right side indicating it is the application in the foreground (on top of all other applications), and the triangle on the left side indicating there's only one window associated with Firefox at this time.

Adding and removing applications from the Launcher

There are two ways to add an application to the Launcher:

- Open the Dash, find the application to add, and drag and drop it to the Launcher
- Run the application you want to add to the Launcher, right-click on the application's icon on the Launcher, and select **Lock to Launcher**.

To remove an application from the Launcher, right-click on the application's icon, then select **Unlock from Launcher**.

The Dash

The Dash is a tool to help you access and find applications and files on your computer quickly. If you are a Windows user, you'll find the Dash to be a more advanced *Start Menu*. If you are a Mac user, the Dash is similar to Launchpad in the dock. If you've used a previous version of Ubuntu or another GNOME Linux distribution, the Dash replaces the GNOME 2 menus. To explore the Dash, click on the top-most icon on the Launcher; the icon has the Ubuntu logo on it. After selecting the Dash icon, another window will appear with a search bar on the top as well as grouping of recently accessed applications, files, and downloads. The search bar provides dynamic results as you enter your search terms. The eight lenses at the bottom are links to your *Home* lens, *Applications* lens, *Wikipedia* lens, *Files and Folders* lens, *Social* lens, *Music* lens, *Photo* lens, and *Videos* lens. Lenses act as specialized search categories in the Dash.

The Dash allows you to search for information, both locally (installed applications, recent files, bookmarks, etc.) as well as remotely (Twitter, Google Docs, etc.). This is accomplished by utilizing one or more lenses, each responsible for providing a category of search results for the Dash. For more information about the Dash and its lenses, see: https://wiki.ubuntu.com/Unity.

There are many sites now on the Internet dedicated to creating and releasing lenses for the Ubuntu Unity desktop. Some sites even teach you how to make your own lenses and maximize the efficencies of the Ubuntu Unity interface.

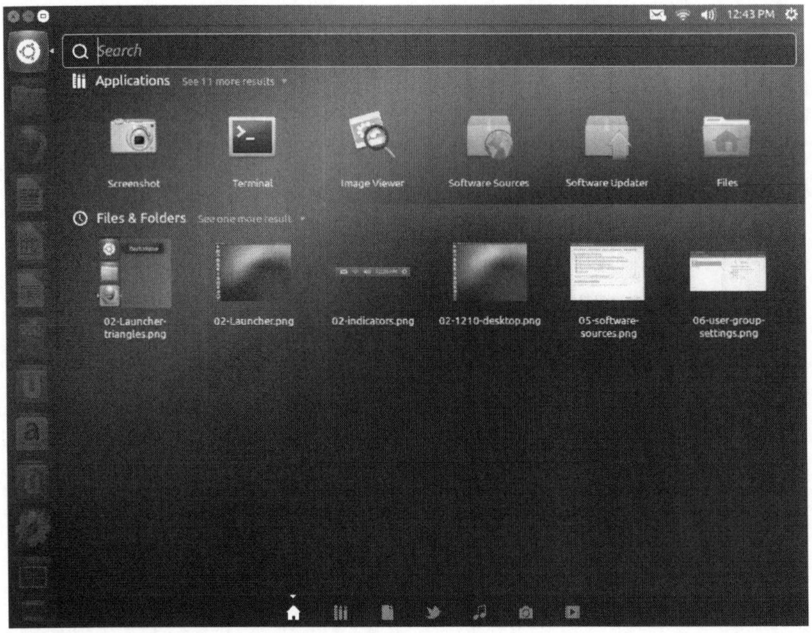

Figure 2.5: The Dash

Search for files and applications with the Dash

The Dash is an extremely powerful tool allowing you to search your entire system for applications and files based on your search terms.

Find files/folder

Dash can help you find the names of files or folders. Simply type in what you remember of the name of the file or folder, and as you type, results will appear in the Dash. The *Files* lens can also assist you in finding files or folders. The *Files* lens shows you the most recent files accessed, as well as recent downloads. You can use the *filter results* button in the top-right corner of the Dash to filter results to your requirements by file or folder modification times, by file type (.odt, .pdf, .doc, .tex, etc.), or by size.

Find applications

The standard Ubuntu installation comes with many applications. Users can also download thousands more applications from the Ubuntu Software Center. As you collect an arsenal of awesome applications (and get a bonus point for alliteration!), it may become difficult to remember the name of a particular application. Simply use the *Application lens* on the Dash. This lens will automatically categorize installed applications under "Recently Used," "Installed," or "Apps Available for Download." You can also enter a name of the application (or a part of it), in the search bar in the Dash, and the names of applications matching your search criteria will appear. Even if you don't remember the name of the application at all, type a keyword that is relevant to that application, and the Dash will find it. For example, type **music**, and the Dash will show you the default music player and any music player you've used).

Ubuntu Software Center and software management will be discussed in detail at Chapter 5: Software Management.

If you are new to the world of Ubuntu, be sure to read the Chapter 3: Working with Ubuntu. It will provide you help in choosing the application(s) that suit your needs.

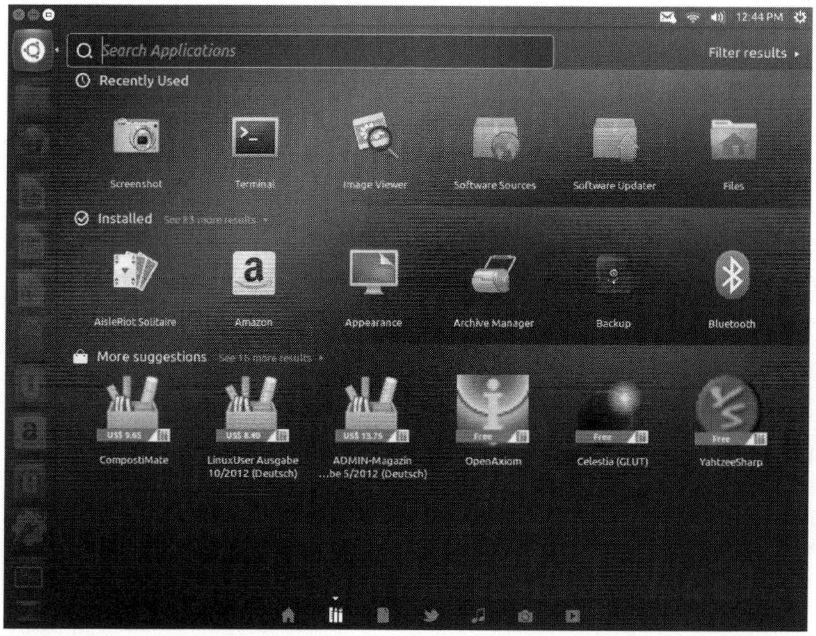

Figure 2.6: You can see the default results when you press Application lens, and also the criteria on the right side.

External search results

In addition to finding applications and files on your local computer using the Dash's search bar, the search criteria is also passed to to the Internet, and results pertinent to your search criteria are return in the Dash. This is a new feature in Ubuntu with the release of 12.10. If you are concerned about local search terms being sent to external resources, you can use the "kill switch" provided in the privacy section of the System Settings to disable all online search results.

 *The online search results within the Dash are turned on by default during installation. If you do not want external search results, go to **System Settings▸Privacy▸Search Results** and switch off the "include online search results" switch.*

Workspaces

Workspaces are also known as virtual desktops. These separate views of your desktop allow you to group applications together, and by doing so, help to reduce clutter and improve desktop navigation. For example, in one workspace, you can open all of your media applications; your office suite in another, and your web browser open in a third workspace. Ubuntu has four workspaces by default.

Switching between workspaces

To switch between workspaces, click on the workspace switcher located on the Launcher. This utility allows you to toggle through the workspaces (whether they contain open applications or not), and choose the one you want to use.

Managing windows

When opening a program in Ubuntu (such as a web browser or a text editor —see Chapter 3: Working with Ubuntu for more information on using applications)—a *window* will appear on your desktop. The windows in Ubuntu are very similar to those in Microsoft Windows or Mac OS X. Simply stated, a window is the box that appears on your screen when you start a program. In Ubuntu, the top part of a window (the *titlebar*) will have the name of the application to the left (most often, the title will be the name of the application). A window will also have three buttons in the top-left corner. From left to right, these buttons represent *close, minimize* window, and *maximize* window. Other window management options are available by right-clicking anywhere on the title bar.

Closing, maximizing, restoring, and minimizing windows

To close a window, click on the ● in the upper-left corner of the window —the first button on the left-hand side. The button immediately to the right of the ● is the minimize button (●) which removes the window from the visible screen and places it in the Launcher. This button doesn't close the application, it just hides the application from view. When an application is minimized to the Launcher, the left-side of the icon in the Launcher will display a triangle showing you the application is still running. Clicking the icon of the application that is minimized will restore the window to its original position. Finally, the right-most button (●) is the *maximize* button, which makes the application window fill the entire screen. Clicking

Figure 2.7: This is the top bar of a window, named *titlebar*. The close, minimize, and maximize buttons are on the top-left corner of window.

the *maximize* button again will return the window to its original size. If a window is maximized, its top-left buttons and menu are automatically hidden from view. To make them appear, just move your mouse to the *menu bar*.

Moving and resizing windows

To move a window around the workspace, place the mouse pointer over the window's titlebar, then click and drag the window while continuing to hold down the left mouse button. To resize a window, place the pointer on an edge or corner of the window so that the pointer turns into a larger, two-sided arrow, (known as the resize icon). You can then click and drag to resize the window.

Switching between open windows

In Ubuntu there are many ways to switch between open windows.

1. If the window is visible on your screen, you can click any portion of it to raise it above all other windows.
2. Use Alt+Tab to select the window you wish to work with. Hold down the Alt key, and keep pressing Tab until the window you're looking for appears in the popup.
3. Click on the corresponding icon on the Launcher. Move your mouse to the left side of your screen to show the Launcher, and right-click on the application icon. If the application has multiple windows open, double-click on the icon in order to select the window you want.

Moving a window to different workspace

To move a window to a different workspace, make sure the window isn't maximized. If it is maximized, click on the right-most button on the left side of the titlebar to restore it to its original size. Then right-click on the window's titlebar and select:

- **Move to Workspace Left**, to move the window to the left workspace
- **Move to Workspace Right**, to move the window to the right workspace
- **Move to Another Workspace**, and then choose the workspace you wish to move the window to.

Window always on the top or on visible workspace

At times, you may want to have a *window always on top* so that it can be seen or monitored while you work with other applications. For example, you may want to browse the web and, at the same time, view and answer to any incoming instant message. To keep a window on top, right-click on the window's titlebar, then select **Always On Top**. Note that this window will be on the top of all windows that are opened in the current workspace. If you want to have a window always on the top regardless of the workspace, right-click on the window's titlebar, then select **Always on Visible Workspace**. This window will now be on top of all other windows across all workspaces.

You can also move a window by holding the Alt key and dragging the window.

Figure 2.8: The *workspace switcher* on the Launcher.

Press Strg+Super+D to hide all window and display the desktop, the same works to restore all windows.

Browsing files on your computer

There are two ways to locate files on your computer—either search for them or access them directly from their folder. You can search for a file via the Dash or **Files & Folders** in the Launcher. You can also use the **Files & Folders** tool to access commonly used folders (such as **Documents**, **Music**, **Downloads**), as well as most recently accessed files.

You can open your Home folder from the Launcher.

Go

To access **Go**, move your mouse over the top bar and select **Go**. The **Go** menu holds a list of commonly used folders (such as **Documents**, **Music**, **Downloads**, and the **Home Folder**). You can browse the files on your computer by clicking **Computer** in this menu. If you set up a home network, you will find a menu item to access shared files or folders.

If you do not see the desktop menu, click somewhere on the desktop and it will appear.

Your Home Folder

The home folder is used to store your personal files. Your home folder matches your login name. When you open your personal folder, you will see there are several more folders inside, including Desktop (which contains any files that are visible on the desktop), Documents, Downloads, Music, Pictures, Public, Templates, and Videos. These are created automatically during the installation process. You can add more files and folders as needed at any time.

Nautilus file manager

Just as Windows has Windows Explorer and Mac os x has Finder to browse files and folders, Ubuntu uses the Nautilus file manager by default.

The Nautilus file manager window

When you select the **Home Folder** shortcut in the Launcher, click on a folder in the Dash, or double-click on a folder on the desktop, the Nautilus file manager window opens. The default window contains the following features:

menu bar The menu bar is located at the top of the screen, the so called global menu. These menus allow you to modify the layout of the browser, navigate, bookmark commonly used folders and files, and view hidden folders and files.

titlebar The titlebar shows the name of the currently selected folder. It also contains the **Close**, **Minimize**, and **Maximize** buttons.

toolbar The toolbar contains tools for navigation. On the right is the search icon (which looks like a magnifying glass); clicking on this icon opens a field so you can search for a file or folder by name. Just below the toolbar, you will see a representation of your current browsing. This is similar to the history function in most browsers; it keeps track of where you are and allows you to backtrack if necessary. You can click on the locations to navigate back through the file browser.

left pane The left pane of the file browser has shortcuts to commonly used folders. When a folder is bookmarked, it appears in the left pane. No matter what folder is open, the left pane will always contain the same folders. This left pane can be changed to display different features (such

If you bookmark a folder, it will appear in the **Bookmarks** menu and in the left pane.

If you start typing a location in the toolbar starting with a / character, Nautilus will automatically change the navigation buttons into a text field labeled *Location*. It is also possible to convert the navigation buttons into a text field by pressing Ctrl+L.

as Information, Tree, History, etc.) by clicking the down arrow beside "Places" near the top.

central pane The largest pane shows the files and folders in the directory that you are currently browsing.

Figure 2.9: Nautilus file manager displaying your home folder.

Navigating Nautilus

To navigate between folders, use the bookmarks in the left pane of the Nautilus file manager. You can also retrace your steps by clicking on the name of a folder in the path bar. Double-clicking on a visible folder will cause you to navigate to it.

What is a Directory? Or a Folder? A directory is a division of space in a file system that you can use to organize files. A folder is the name given to a directory in a Graphical User Interface (GUI) environment like Nautilus.

Opening files

A file, in its simplest form, is data. Data can represent a text document, database information, or data that will be used to produce music or video. To open a file, you can either double-click on its icon or right-click the icon and select one of the **Open With** options. Ubuntu attempts to determine what application to use for the file being opened, and most of the time, Ubuntu chooses correctly. However, if you want to open the file using an application other than what is selected, then choose **Open With Other Application**. A selection of installed applications will appear. Make your selection, and the file will open in the selected application.

Creating new folders

To create a new folder from within Nautilus, click **File ▸ Create New Folder**. Then, name the folder that appears by replacing the default "Untitled Folder" with your desired label (*e.g.*, "Personal Finances"). You can also create a new folder by pressing Ctrl+Shift+N, or by right-clicking in the file browser window and selecting **Create New Folder** from the popup menu (this action will also work on the desktop).

Hidden Files and Folders

If you wish to hide certain folders or files, place a dot (.) in front of the name (*e.g.*, ".Personal Finances"). In some cases it is impossible to hide files and folders without prefixing them with a dot. In Nautilus, these folders can be hidden by creating a .hidden file. This is accomplished by opening the file and typing the name of the file or folder you wish to hide. Make sure that each file or folder is on a separate line. When you open Nautilus, the folder will no longer be visible.

You can easily view hidden files by clicking **View ▸ Show Hidden Files** or by pressing Ctrl+H. Hiding files with a dot (.) is *not* a security measure—it simply provides a way to keep folders organized and tidy.

Copying and moving files and folders

You can copy files or folders in Nautilus by clicking **Edit ▸ Copy**, or by right-clicking on the item and selecting **Copy** from the popup menu. When using the **Edit** menu in Nautilus, make sure you've selected the file or folder you want to copy first (by left-clicking on it once). Multiple files can be selected by left-clicking in an empty space (*i.e.*, not on a file or folder), holding the mouse button down, and dragging the cursor across the desired files or folders. This "click-drag" move is useful when you are selecting items that are grouped closely together. To select multiple files or folders that are not positioned next to each other, hold down the Ctrl key while clicking on each item individually. Once multiple files and/or folders are selected, you can use the **Edit** menu to perform actions just like you would for a single item. When one or more items have been "copied," navigate to the desired location then click **Edit ▸ Paste** (or right-click in an empty area of the window and select **Paste**) to copy them to the new location. While the *copy* command can be used to make a duplicate of a file or folder in a new location, the *cut* command can be used to move files and folders around. That is, a copy will be placed in a new location, and the original will be removed from its current location. To move a file or folder, select the item you want to move then click **Edit ▸ Cut**. Navigate to the desired location, then click **Edit ▸ Paste**. As with the *copy* command above, you can also perform this action using the right-click menu, and it will work for multiple files or folders at once. An alternative way to move a file or folder is to click on the item, and then drag it to the new location.

> You can also use the keyboard shortcuts Ctrl+X, Ctrl+C and Ctrl+V to cut, copy, and paste (respectively) files and folders.

> When you "cut" or "copy" a file or folder, nothing will happen until you "paste" it somewhere. Paste will only affect the most recent item that was cut or copied.

> In the Nautilus **Edit** menu, you will also find the **Copy To** and **Move To** buttons. These can be used to copy or move items to common locations and can be useful if you are using panes (see below). Note that it is unnecessary to use **Paste** when using these options.

> If you click on a file or folder, drag it, and then hold down the Alt key and drop it to your destination folder, a menu will appear asking whether you want to *copy*, *move*, or *link* the item. Notice that the symbol of the mouse cursor changes from an arrow into a question mark as soon as you hold down the Alt key.

Using multiple tabs and multiple Nautilus windows

Opening multiple Nautilus windows can be useful for dragging files and folders between locations. The option of *tabs* (as well as *panes*) is also available in Nautilus. To open a second windows when browsing a folder in Nautilus, select **File ▸ New Window** or press Ctrl+N. This will open a new window, allowing you to drag files and/or folders between two locations. To open a new tab, click **File ▸ New Tab** or press Ctrl+T. A new row will appear above the space used for browsing your files containing two tabs—both will display the directory you were originally browsing. You can click these tabs to switch between them to click and drag files or folders between tabs the same as you would between windows. You can also open a second pane in Nautilus so you can see two locations at once without having to switch between tabs or windows. To open a second pane, click **View ▸ Extra Pane**, or press F3 on your keyboard. Again, dragging files and folders between panes is a quick way to move or copy items.

> When dragging items between Nautilus windows, tabs, or panes, a small symbol will appear over the mouse cursor to let you know which action will be performed when you release the mouse button. A plus sign (+) indicates you are about to copy the item, whereas a small arrow means the item will be moved. The default action will depend on the folders you are using.

Searching for files and folders on your computer

You can search for files and folders using the Dash or Nautilus.

> Search for files and folders quickly by pressing Ctrl+F in Nautilus and then typing what you want to find.

Search using the Dash

In the Dash, simply type your search terms in the search bar at the top of the Dash.

Alternatively, you may use the **Search for Files and folders** lens; here you can use a filter to narrow down your search. Open the drop-down menu on the right side of the search bar. Select *Last modified*, *Type*, *e.g.*,

Documents, or *Size*. It is sufficient to type the first few letters of the file or folder you are searching for.

Search using Nautilus

In Nautilus, click **Go ▸ Search for Files**, or press `Ctrl+F`. This opens the search field where you can type the name of the file or folder you want to find.

Customizing your desktop

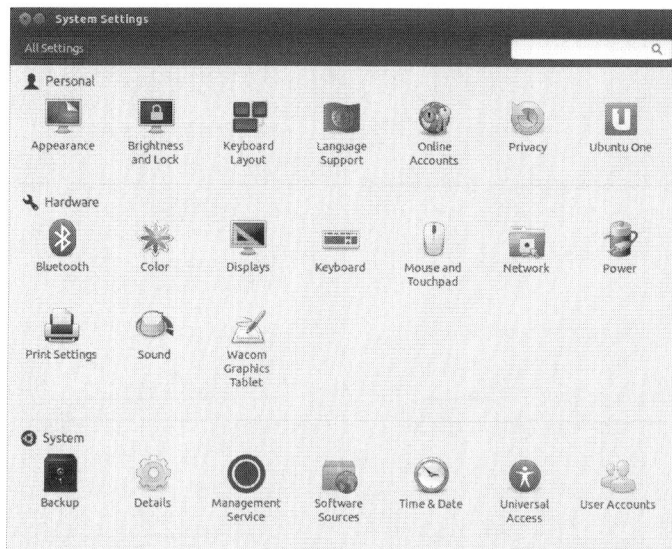

Figure 2.10: You can change most of your system's settings here.

One of the advantages to a windowed environment through Unity is the ability to change the look and feel of your desktop. Don't like the default Ubuntu theme? Do you have a picture of your third cousin's aunt's uncle's nephew's pet chihuahua that you'd love to see on your desktop as wallpaper? All of this (and more) is possible through desktop customizations in Unity. Most customizations can be reached via the Session Indicator and then selecting **System Settings** to open the System Settings application window. The Dash, desktop appearance, themes, wallpapers, accessibility, and other configuration settings are available here. For more information see Session options.

Appearance

You can change the background, fonts, and window theme to further modify the look and feel of your desktop. To begin, open Appearance by either right-clicking on your background and selecting **Change Desktop Background** or selecting **Session Indicator ▸ System Settings ▸ Appearance**.

Theme

The "Appearance" window will display the current selected background wallpaper and theme. Themes control the appearance of your windows, buttons, scroll bars, panels, icons, and other parts of the desktop. The *Ambiance* theme is used by default, but there are other themes from which you

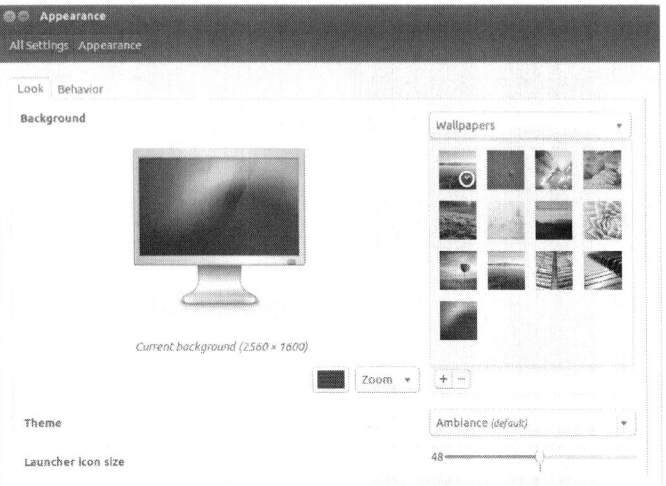

Figure 2.11: You can change the theme in the **Look** tab of the "Appearance" window.

can choose. Just click once on any of the listed themes to give a new theme a try. The theme will change your desktop appearance immediately.

Desktop background

Under **Background**, you may choose from **Wallpapers**, **Pictures Folder**, and **Colors and Gradients**. When **Wallpapers** is selected, you will see Ubuntu's default selection of backgrounds. To change the background simply click the picture you would like to use. You're not limited to this selection though. To use one of your own pictures, click the +... button, and navigate to the image you would like to use, double-click the image, and the change will take effect immediately. This image will then be added to your list of available backgrounds. If you want to choose from a larger selection of desktop backgrounds, click the "Get More Backgrounds Online" link at the bottom of the "Appearance Preferences" window. This link will open your web browser, and direct you to the http://art.gnome.org/backgrounds website.

Accessibility

Ubuntu has built-in tools that make using the computer easier for people with certain physical limitations. You can find these tools by opening the Dash and searching for "Universal Access." On the **Seeing** tab you can manage the text size, the contrast of the interfaces, enable a zoom tool and even a screen reader. Selecting high-contrast themes and larger on-screen fonts can assist those with vision difficulties. You can activate "Visual Alerts" though the **Hearing** tab, if you have hearing impairment. Also you can adjust keyboard and mouse settings to suit your needs through the **Typing** and **Pointing and Clicking** tabs respectively.

Orca screen reader

Orca is a useful tool for people with visual impairments. Orca comes preinstalled in Ubuntu. To run Orca, click on the Dash, type **Orca**, and click on the displayed result. Orca is the "Screen Reader" part of Universal Access and can be launched once the "Screen Reader" is activated. Orca's voice synthesizer will activate and assist you through the various options

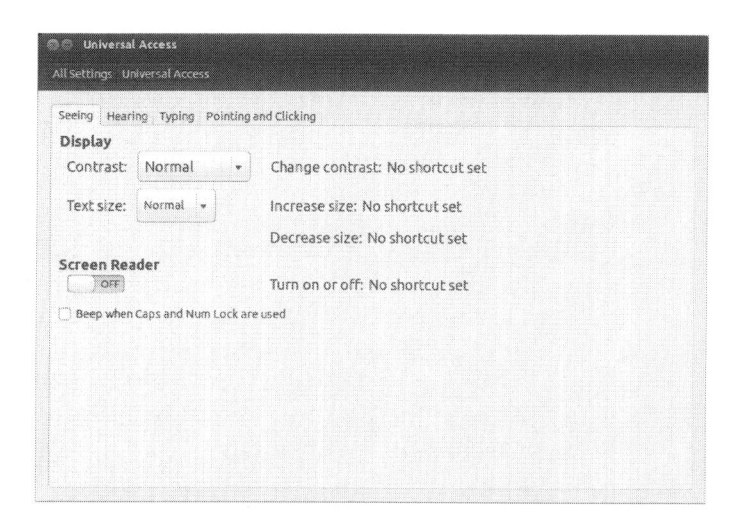

Figure 2.12: Universal allows you to enable extra features to make it easier to use your computer.

such as voice type, voice language, Braille, and screen magnification. Once you have finished selecting your settings, you will need to log out of the computer (Orca will offer to do this for you). When you log back in, the Orca settings you selected will automatically run every time you use your computer.

Session options

When you have finished working on your computer, you can choose to log out, suspend, restart, or shut down through the **Session Indicator** on the far right side of the top panel.

Logging out

Logging out will leave the computer running but return you to the login screen. This is useful for switching between users, such as when a different person wishes to log in to their account, or if you are ever instructed to "log out and back in again."

You can also log out by pressing the Ctrl+Alt+Del keys.

Before logging out, you should always verify your work in any open applications is saved.

Suspend

To save energy, you can put your computer into *suspend mode*, which will save its current condition to internal memory, power off all devices, and allow you to start back up more quickly. While in a suspended state, the computer will use just a trickle of energy; this is required because the session is saved to internal memory, and if no power goes to internal memory, the data will be lost.

Rebooting

To reboot your computer, select **Shut Down…** from the "Session Indicator" and click on **Restart**.

Shut down

To totally power down your computer, select **Shut Down…** from the "Session Indicator" and click on **Shutdown**.

Other options

From the **Session Indicator**, you can select **Lock Screen** to require a password before using the computer again—this is useful if you need to leave your computer for some duration. You can also use the **Session Indicator** to set up a guest session for a friend, or to *switch users* to log into another user account without closing your applications.

You can lock your screen quickly by using the keyboard shortcut `Ctrl+Alt+L`. Locking your screen is recommended if you move away from your computer for a short amount of time.

Getting help

General Help

Ubuntu, just like other operating systems, has a built-in help reference called the Ubuntu Desktop Guide. To access it, click on the Dash and type `Help`. Alternatively, you can press F1 while on the desktop, or select **Ubuntu Help** from the **Help** menu in the menu bar.

Many applications have their own help section which can be accessed by clicking the **Help** menu within the application window.

Heads-Up Display help

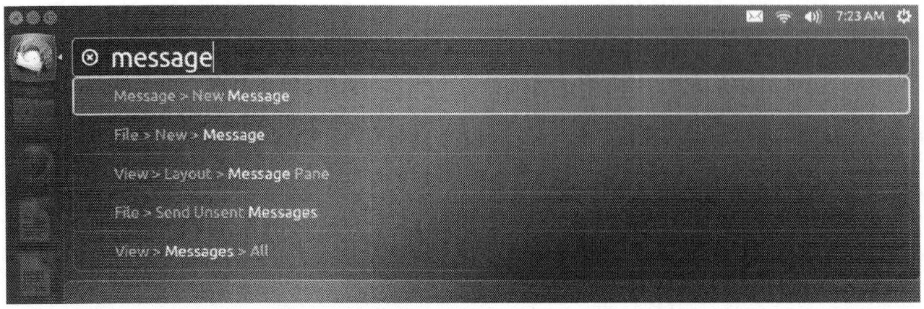

Figure 2.13: The HUD (heads-up display) shows application-specific help information based on your general input.

The HUD (heads-up display) is a new help feature introduced in Ubuntu 12.04. This is a keyboard-friendly utility to help you find commands, features, and preferences embedded deep within the menu structure of an application. Activate the HUD by pressing the left Alt key on the keyboard. If you want to search a menu item, such as creating a new message in Thunderbird, then just type *message* in the HUD and the option for composing a new email message will come up in the list of matching results. You can press the Enter key to active the command. The HUD works for almost all applications that are natively installable in Ubuntu; it also works for some applications running under WINE.

The HUD feature may not be available in all applications as this is a new capability in Ubuntu 12.04. Your mileage may vary!

WINE is an acronym for *Wine Is Not an Emulator*. It allows you to run some Windows-based applications in Ubuntu. Discussion of how to use WINE is beyond the scope of this manual, but it is worth checking out if you need to run Windows applications under Ubuntu.

Online Help

If you can't find an answer to your question in this manual or in the Ubuntu Desktop Guide, you can contact the Ubuntu community through the Ubuntu Forums (http://ubuntuforums.org). Many Ubuntu users open an account on the forums to receive help, and in turn provide support to others as they gain more knowledge. Another useful resource is the Ubuntu Wiki (https://wiki.ubuntu.com), a website maintained by the Ubuntu community.

We encourage you to check any information you find on other websites with multiple sources when possible, but only follow directions if you understand them completely.

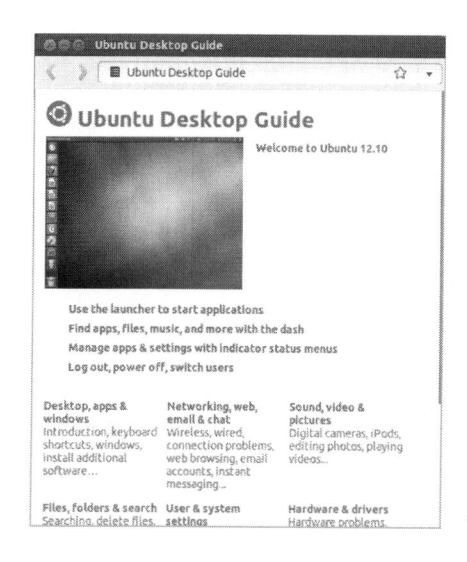

Figure 2.14: The built-in system help provides topic-based help for Ubuntu.

3 Working with Ubuntu

All the applications you need

If you are migrating from a Windows or Mac platform, you may wonder if the programs that you once used are available for Ubuntu. Some of the programs you already use have native Linux versions. And, for those that don't, there are free and open-source applications that will cover your needs. This section will recommend some alternates that will work well on Ubuntu. Most of the applications listed in this section are available via the Software Center. Those followed by an asterisk (*) can be downloaded directly from their official websites.

You can search for more applications in the Ubuntu Software Center by the category that you are interested in.

Office Suites

- Windows: Microsoft Office, LibreOffice
- Mac OS X: iWork, Microsoft Office, LibreOffice
- Linux: LibreOffice, KOffice, GNOME Office, Kexi (database application)

In Ubuntu you may choose among many office suites. The most popular suite is the LibreOffice (formerly OpenOffice). Included in the suite:

- Writer—word processor
- Calc—spreadsheet
- Impress—presentation manager
- Draw—drawing program
- Base—database
- Math—equation editor

LibreOffice Suite is installed by default. Note that Base is not installed by default and it can be installed through Ubuntu Software Center.

Email Applications

- Windows: Microsoft Outlook, Mozilla Thunderbird
- Mac OS X: Mail.app, Microsoft Outlook, Mozilla Thunderbird
- Linux: Mozilla Thunderbird, Evolution, KMail

As with office suites, there are multiple options for email applications. One very popular email application is Mozilla Thunderbird, which is also available for Windows. Thunderbird is the default email application in Ubuntu. Another option is Evolution—similar to Microsoft Outlook, it also provides a calendar.

Web Browsers

- Windows: Microsoft Internet Explorer, Mozilla Firefox, Opera, Chromium, Google Chrome
- Mac OS X: Safari, Mozilla Firefox, Opera, Chromium, Google Chrome
- Linux: Mozilla Firefox, Opera,* Chromium, Google Chrome,* Epiphany

The most popular web browsers can be installed directly from the Ubuntu Software Center.

Opera is available for download from http://www.opera.com/browser/download/. Google Chrome is available for download from https://www.google.com/chrome/.

PDF Readers

- Windows: Adobe Reader
- Mac OS X: Adobe Reader
- Linux: Evince, Adobe Reader, Okular

Evince is a user-friendly and minimalistic reader, and it is the default PDF reader. If Evince doesn't cover your needs, Adobe Reader is available for Ubuntu too.

Multimedia Players

- Windows: Windows Media Player, VLC
- Mac OS X: Quicktime, VLC
- Linux: Totem, VLC, MPlayer, Kaffeine

For multimedia, Ubuntu users have a wide variety of options for high quality players. Two popular and powerful media players for Ubuntu are VLC and Mplayer. Meanwhile, the classic and user-friendly Totem is the default media player in Ubuntu.

Music Players and Podcatchers

- Windows: Windows Media Player, iTunes, Winamp
- Mac OS X: iTunes
- Linux: Rhythmbox, Banshee, Amarok, Audacity, Miro

There are several options for listening to music with Ubuntu: Rhythmbox (installed by default) and Amarok among many others. With these you can listen to music and your favorite podcasts. Audacity is similar to Winamp. There is Miro for those of you who watch video podcasts and TV series from the Internet.

CD/DVD Burning

- Windows: Nero Burning ROM, InfraRecorder
- Mac OS X: Burn, Toast Titanium
- Linux: Brasero, K3b, Gnome-baker

There are several popular disk burning applications such as Gnome-baker, Brasero, Ubuntu's default CD burner, and K3b. These burners are powerful tools, offering user-friendly interfaces, many features and they are all open source and free of charge!

Photo Management

- Windows: Microsoft Office Picture Manager, Picasa
- Mac OS X: Aperture, Picasa
- Linux: Shotwell, gThumb, Gwenview, F-Spot

You can view and manage your favorite photos with Shotwell, Ubuntu's default photo manager, or with gThumb, Gwenview, and F-Spot.

Graphics Editors

- Windows: Adobe Photoshop, GIMP

- Mac os x: Adobe Photoshop, GIMP
- Linux: GIMP, Inkscape

GIMP is a very powerful graphics editor. You can create your own graphics, taper your photographs, modify your pictures. GIMP, a powerful alternative to Photoshop, covers the needs of novice users, professional photographers, and designers.

⚠️ *GIMP is not loaded by default, but can be installed via the Software Center.*

Instant Messaging

- Windows: Windows Live Messenger, AIM, Yahoo! Messenger, Google Talk
- Mac os x: Windows Live Messenger, AIM, Yahoo! Messenger, Adium, iChat
- Linux: Empathy, Pidgin, Kopete, aMSN

None of the other platform IM clients have Linux versions. However, you can use Pidgin, Empathy or Kopete to communicate over most protocols including: AIM, MSN, Google Talk (Jabber/XMPP), Facebook, Yahoo!, and ICQ. This means you need only one client to communicate with all of your friends. The drawback is that some of these clients have limited video support. If you are using MSN exclusively, aMSN may be worth a try.

VoIP Applications

- Windows: Skype, Google Video Chat
- Mac os x: Skype, Google Video Chat
- Linux: Ekiga, Skype, Google Video Chat

VoIP technologies allow you to talk to people over the Internet. The most popular such application is Skype, which is available for Linux. An open-source alternative Ekiga supports voice communication using the SIP protocol. Note that Ekiga isn't compatible with Skype.

BitTorrent Clients

- Windows: μTorrent, Azureus
- Mac os x: Transmission, Azureus
- Linux: Transmission, Deluge, Azureus, KTorrent, Flush, Vuze, BitStorm Lite

There are a number of BitTorrent clients for Ubuntu: Transmission, Ubuntu's default client, is simple and light-weight, Deluge, Azureus and KTorrent offer many features and can satisfy the most demanding of users.

Getting online

This section of the manual will help you to check your connection to the Internet and help you configure it where needed. Ubuntu can connect to the Internet using a wired, wireless, or dialup connection. Ubuntu also supports more advanced connection methods, which will be briefly discussed at the end of this section.

A wired connection is when your computer connects to the Internet using an Ethernet cable. This is usually connected to a wall socket or a networking device—like a switch or a router.

A wireless connection is when your computer connects to the Internet using a wireless radio network—usually known as Wi-Fi. Most routers now come with wireless capability, as do most laptops and netbooks. Because of this, Wi-Fi is the most common connection type for these types of devices. Wireless connectivity makes laptops and netbooks more portable when moving to different rooms of a house and while traveling.

A dialup connection is when your computer uses a *modem* to connect to the Internet through a telephone line.

In order to connect wirelessly, you must be in a location with a working wireless network. To set up your own wireless network, you will need to purchase and install a wireless router or access point. Some locations may already have a publicly accessible wireless networks available. If you are unsure whether your computer has a wireless card, check with your manufacturer.

NetworkManager

In order to connect to the Internet using Ubuntu, you need to use the NetworkManager utility. NetworkManager allows you to turn network connections on or off, manage wired and wireless networks, and make other network connections, such as dial up, mobile broadband, and VPNs.

You can access NetworkManager by using its icon found the top panel. This icon may look different depending on your current connection state. Clicking this icon will reveal a list of available network connections. The current connection (if any) will have the word "disconnect" underneath it. You can click on "disconnect" to manually disconnect from that network.

This menu also allows you to view technical details about your current connection or edit all connection settings. In the image to the right you will see a check mark next to "Enable Networking." Deselect "Enable Networking" to disable all network connections. Select "Enable Networking" to enable networking again. This can be very useful when you are required to turn off all wireless communications, like in an airplane.

Figure 3.1: The network connection states: (a) disconnected, (b) wired, and (c) wireless.

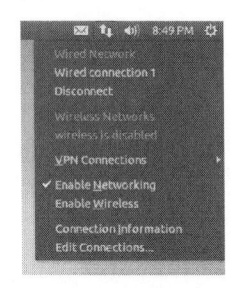

Figure 3.2: Here you can see the currently active connection is "Wired connection 1."

Establishing a wired connection

If you have an *Ethernet* cable running from a wall socket or networking device, such as a switch or router, then you will want to setup a wired connection in Ubuntu.

In order to connect to the Internet with a wired connection, you need to know whether your network supports DHCP *(Dynamic Host Configuration Protocol)*. DHCP is a way for your computer to automatically be configured to access your network and/or Internet connection. DHCP is usually automatically configured on your router. This is usually the quickest and easiest way of establishing a connection to the Internet. If you are unsure whether your router is setup to use DHCP, you may wish to contact your ISP's *(Internet Service Provider)* customer service line to check. If your router isn't configured to use DHCP then they will also be able to tell you what configuration settings you need in order to get online.

Are you already online? If the NetworkManager icon in the top panel shows a connection then you may have successfully connected during the Ubuntu setup process. You can also simply open a browser and see if you have access to the Internet. If so, you do not need to do anything for the rest of this section.

Automatic connections with DHCP

If your network supports DHCP then you may already be set up for online access. To check this, click on the NetworkManager icon. There should be a "Wired Network" heading in the menu. If "Wired connection 1" appears directly underneath, then your machine is currently connected and probably setup for DHCP. If "Disconnected" appears in gray underneath the wired network section, look below to see if an option labeled "Wired connec-

Figure 3.3: This window displays your IP address and other connection information.

tion 1" appears in the list. If so, click on it to attempt to establish a wired connection.

To check if you are online, click on the NetworkManager icon in the top panel and select the Connection Information option. You should see a window showing details of your connection. If your IP address is displayed as 0.0.0.0 or starts with 169.254, then your computer was not successfully assigned connection information through DHCP. If it shows another address (*e.g.*, 192.168.219.133), then it is likely that your DHCP connection to the router was successful. To test your Internet connection, you may want to open the Firefox web browser to try loading a web page. More information on using Firefox can be found later in this chapter.

Manual configuration with static address

If your network does not support DHCP then you need to know a few items of information before you can get online. If you do not know any of this information, then you call your ISP.

- An *IP address*—This is a unique address used for identifying your computer on the network. An IP address is always given in four numbered groups, separated by dots, for example, 192.168.100.10. When connecting using DHCP, this address will periodically change (hence, the name "dynamic"). However, if you have configured a static IP address, your IP address will never change.
- A *network mask*—This tells your computer the size of the network to which it is being connected. It is formatted the same way as the IP address, but usually looks something like 255.255.255.0.
- A *gateway*—This is the IP address of the device that your machine looks to for access to the Internet. Usually, this will be the router's IP address.
- *DNS server*—This is the IP address of the DNS *(Domain Name Service)* server. DNS is what your computer uses to resolve IP addresses to domain names. For example http://www.ubuntu.com resolves to 91.189.94.156. This is the IP address of the Ubuntu website on the Internet. DNS is used so you don't have to remember IP addresses. Domain names (like ubuntu.com) are much easier to remember. You will need at least one DNS server address but you can enter up to three addresses in case one server is unavailable.

To manually configure a wired connection, click on the NetworkManager icon and select **Edit Connections**. Make sure you are looking at the "Wired" tab inside the "Network Connections" window. The list may already have an entry, such as "Wired connection 1" or a similar name. If a connection is listed, select it and click the **Edit** button. If no connection is listed, click the **Add** button.

If you are adding a connection, you need to provide a name for the connection. This will distinguish the connection being added from any other connections added in future. In the "Connection Name" field, choose a name such as "Wired Home."

To setup the connection:

1. Make sure that the **Connect automatically** option is selected under the connection name.
2. Switch to the **IPv4 Settings** tab.
3. Change the **Method** to "Manual."
4. Click on the **Add** button next to the empty list of addresses.

An IP (Internet Protocol) address is a unique number assigned to your machine so that your router can identify you on the network. Think of it like a phone number for your computer. Having this unique address allows the router to speak to your computer, and therefore send/receive data.
If you are still not online after following these steps, you may need to try setting up your network connection manually using a static IP address.

If you do not know your ISP's DNS server addresses, Google has DNS servers that anyone in the world can use for free. The addresses of these servers are: Primary—8.8.8.8 Secondary—8.8.4.4

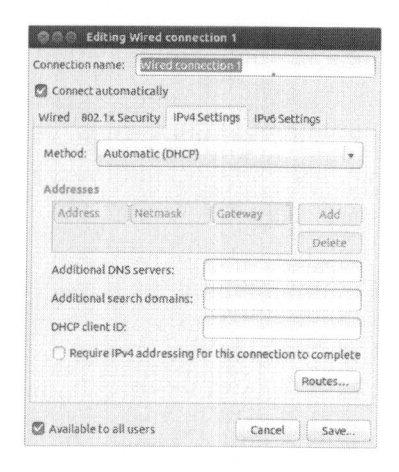

Figure 3.4: In this window you can manually edit a connection.

5. Enter your IP address in the field below the **Address** header.
6. Click to the right of the IP address, directly below the **Netmask** header and enter your network mask. If you are unsure, "255.255.255.0" is the most common.
7. Click on the right of the network mask directly below the **Gateway** header and enter the address of your gateway.
8. In the **DNS Servers** field below, enter the address of your DNS server(s). If you are entering more than one, separate them with commas—for example, "8.8.8.8, 8.8.4.4".
9. Click **Save** to save your changes.

When you have returned to the Network Connections screen, your newly added connection should now be listed. Click **Close** to return to the desktop. If your connection was configured correctly, the NetworkManager icon should have changed to show an active wired connection. To test if your connection is properly set up, simply open a web browser. If you can access the Internet, then you are connected!

Wireless

If your computer is equipped with a wireless (Wi-Fi) card and you have a wireless network nearby, you should be able to set up a wireless connection in Ubuntu.

Connecting to a wireless network for the first time

If your computer has a wireless network card, you can connect to a wireless network. Most laptops and netbooks have a built-in wireless networking card.

Ubuntu is usually able to detect any wireless network in range of your computer. To see a list of wireless networks, click on the NetworkManager icon. Under the "Wireless Networks" heading you should see a list of available wireless networks. Each network will be shown by its name and a signal meter to the left showing its relative signal strength. The signal meter looks like a set of bars similar to what is seen when viewing signal strength of a cell phone. Simply put, the more bars, the stronger the signal.

A wireless network can be open to anyone, or it can be protected with a password. A small padlock will be displayed by the signal bar if any wireless network within range are password-protected. You will need to know the correct password in order to connect to these secured wireless networks.

To connect to a wireless network, select the desired network by clicking on its name within the list. This will be the name that was used during the installation of the wireless router or access point. Most ISPs (Internet service providers) provide pre-configured routers with a sticker on them detailing the current wireless network name and password. Most publicly accessible wireless networks will be easily identifiable by the name used for the wireless network—for example "Starbucks-Wireless."

If the network is unprotected (*i.e.*, the signal meter does not show a padlock), a connection should be established within a few seconds—and without a password required. The NetworkManager icon in the top panel will animate as Ubuntu attempts to connect to the network. If the connection is successful, the icon will change to display a signal meter. An on-screen

*A MAC address is a hardware address for your computer's network card. Entering this information is sometimes important when using a cable modem connection. If you know the MAC address of your network card, this can be entered in the appropriate text field in the **Wired** tab of the editing window. To find the MAC addresses for all installed networking devices, open a terminal window, and at the command line prompt, type `ifconfig`. This will display a lot of information about each of the network devices installed on the computer. The wired devices will be labeled as **LAN0**, **LAN1**, etc. The wireless devices will appear as **WLAN0**, **WLAN1**, etc.*

To improve speed and reliability of your wireless connection, try moving closer to your router or wireless access point.

notification message will also appear informing you that the connection was successful.

If the network is password-protected, Ubuntu will display a window called "Wireless Network Authentication Required" as it tries to make a connection. This means that a valid password is required to make a connection. This is what the screen should look like:

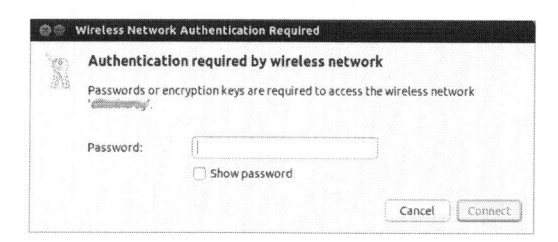

Figure 3.5: Enter your wireless network password.

If you know the password, enter it in the **Password** field and then click on the **Connect** button. As you type the password, it will be obscured from view to prevent others from reading the password as you type it. Once the password is entered, click on the **Connect** button. The NetworkManager icon in the top panel will animate as Ubuntu attempts to connect to the network. If the connection is successful, the icon will change to display a signal meter. An on-screen notification message will also appear informing you that the connection was successful.

To verify the characters you are entering for the password, you can view the password by selecting the **Show Password** check box. Then, you can make the password obscure again by deselecting the **Show password** check box.

If you entered the password incorrectly, or if it doesn't match the correct password (for example if it has recently been changed and you have forgotten), NetworkManager will make another attempt to connect to the network, and the "Wireless Network Authentication Required" window will re-appear so that you can re-type the password. You can hit the **Cancel** button to abort the connection. If you do not know the correct password, you may need to call your ISP's customer support line or contact your network administrator.

Once you have successfully established a wireless connection, Ubuntu will store these settings (including the password) to make it easier to connect to this same wireless network in the future. You may also be prompted to select a *keyring* password here. The keyring stores passwords in one place so you can access them all in the future by remembering just the keyring password.

Connecting to a saved wireless network

Ubuntu will automatically try to connect to a wireless network in range if it has the settings saved. This works on both open and secure wireless networks.

If you have numerous wireless networks in range that are saved on your computer, Ubuntu may choose to connect to one network while you may want to connect to another network. To remedy this action, click on the NetworkManager icon. A list of wireless networks will appear along with their signal meters. Simply click on the network to which you wish to connect, and Ubuntu will disconnect from the current network and attempt to connect to the one you have selected.

If the network is secure and Ubuntu has the details for this network saved, Ubuntu will automatically connect. If the details for this network connection are not saved, are incorrect, or have changed, then you will be prompted to enter the network password again. If the network is open (no password required), all of this will happen automatically and the connection will be established.

Connecting to a hidden wireless network

In some environments, you may need to connect to a hidden wireless network. These hidden networks do not broadcast their names, and, therefore, their names will not appear in the list of available wireless networks even if they are in range. In order to connect to a hidden wireless network, you will need to get its name and security details from your network administrator or ISP.

To connect to a hidden wireless network:

1. Click on NetworkManager in the top panel.
2. Select **Connect to a hidden wireless network**. Ubuntu will then open the "Connect to Hidden Wireless Network" window.
3. In the **Network name** field, enter the name of the network. This is also known as the *SSID (Service Set Identifier)*. You must enter the name exactly how it was given to you. For example, if the name is "Ubuntu-Wireless," entering "ubuntu-wireless" will not work as the "U" and "W" are both uppercase in the correct name.
4. In the **Wireless security** field, select one of the options. If the network is an open network, leave the field set to "None." If you do not know the correct setting for the field, you will not be able to connect to the hidden network.
5. Click the **Connect** button. If the network is secure, you will be prompted for the password. Provided you have entered all of the details correctly, the network should then connect, and you will receive an on-screen notification informing you that the connection was a success.

As is the case with visible wireless networks, hidden wireless network settings will be saved once a connection is made, and the wireless network will then appear in the list of saved connections.

Disabling and enabling your wireless card

By default, wireless access is enabled if you have a wireless card installed in your computer. In certain environments (like on airplanes), you may need to temporarily disable your wireless card.

To disable your wireless card, click on the NetworkManager icon and deselect the **Enable Wireless** option. Your wireless radio will now be turned off, and your computer will no longer search for wireless networks.

To reactivate your wireless card, simply select the **Enable Wireless** option. Ubuntu will then begin to search for wireless networks automatically. If you are in range of a saved network, you will automatically be connected.

Many modern laptops also have a physical switch/button built into the chassis that provides a way to quickly enable/disable the wireless card.

Changing an existing wireless network

At times you may want to change the settings of a saved wireless network —for example, when the wireless password gets changed.

To edit a saved wireless network connection:

1. Click on the NetworkManager icon and select **Edit Connections**…
2. A "Network Connections" window will open. Click on the **Wireless** tab.

3. By default, saved networks are in chronological order with the most recently connected at the top. Find the network you want to edit, select it, and click on the **Edit** button.
4. Ubuntu will now open a window called "Editing ⟨*connection name*⟩", where ⟨*connection name*⟩ is the name of the connection you are editing. This window will display a number of tabs.
5. Above the tabs, there is a field called **Connection name** where you can change the name of the connection to give it a more recognizable name.
6. If the **Connect automatically** option is not selected, Ubuntu will detect the wireless network but will not attempt a connection until it is selected from the NetworkManager menu. Select or deselect this option as needed.
7. On the **Wireless** tab, you may need to edit the SSID field. A SSID is the wireless connection's network name. If this field isn't set correctly, Ubuntu will not be able to connect to the wireless network in question.
8. Below the SSID is a **Mode** field. The "Infrastructure" mode means that you would be connecting to a wireless router or access point. The "ad-hoc" mode is for a computer-to-computer connection (where one computer shares another's connection) and is often only used in advanced cases.
9. On the **Wireless Security** tab, you can change the **Security** field. A selection of "None" means that you are using an open network that doesn't require a password. Other selection in this tab may required additional information:

    WEP 40/128-bit Key is an older security setting still in use by some older wireless devices. If your network uses this method of security, you will need to enter a key in the **Key** field that will appear when this mode is selected.

    WEP 128-bit Passphrase is the same older security as above. However, instead of having a key, your network administrator should have provided you with a passphrase to connect to the network.

    WPA & WPA2 Personal is the most common security mode for wireless networking. Once you select this mode, you will need to enter a password in the **Password** field.

    If your network administrator requires LEAP, Dynamic WEP or WPA & WPA2 Enterprise then you will need to have the administrator help you with those modes.

10. In the **IPv4 Settings** tab, you can change the **Method** field from "Automatic (DHCP)" to "Manual" or one of the other methods. For setting up manual settings (also known as a static address), please see the section above on manual setup for wired network connections.
11. When you finish making changes to the connection, click **Apply** to save your changes and close the window. You can click **Cancel** at any time to close the window without saving any changes.
12. Finally, click **Close** on the "Network Connections" window to return to the desktop.

After clicking **Apply**, any changes made to the network connection will take effect immediately.

Other connection methods

There are other ways to get connected with Ubuntu:

46   GETTING STARTED WITH UBUNTU 12.10

- With NetworkManager, you can configure mobile broadband connections to connect to the Internet through your cellular data carrier.
- You can connect to digital subscriber line (DSL) networks, a method of connecting to the Internet through your phone line via a modem.
- It is also possible for NetworkManager to establish a virtual private network (VPN) connection. These are most commonly used to create a secure connection to a workplace network.

The instructions for making connections using mobile broadband, DSL, or VPN are beyond the scope of this guide.

Browsing the web

Once you have connected to the Internet, you should be able to browse the web. Mozilla Firefox is the default application for this in Ubuntu.

Figure 3.6: The default Ubuntu home page for the Firefox web browser.

Starting Firefox

There are several ways to start Firefox. By default Ubuntu has the Firefox icon within the Launcher (the vertical bar down the left side of the screen). Select this icon to open Firefox. Or, open the Dash (the top-most icon in the Launcher) and search for **firefox** using the search box. If your keyboard has a "www" button, you can press that button to start Firefox.

Navigating web pages

Viewing your homepage

When you start Firefox, you will see your home page. By default, this is the Ubuntu Start Page.

To quickly go to your home page, press Alt+Home on your keyboard or press on the home icon in Firefox.

Navigating to another page

To navigate to a new web page, you need to enter its Internet address (also known as a URL) into the Location Bar. URLs normally begin with "http://" followed by one or more names that identify the address. One example is "http://www.ubuntu.com/." (Normally, you can omit the "http://" part. Firefox will fill it in for you.)

URL stands for uniform resource locator, which tells the computer how to find something on the Internet—such as a document, web page or an email address. WWW stands for World Wide Web, which means the web pages by which most people interact with the Internet.

Figure 3.7: You can enter a web address or search the Internet by typing in the location bar.

To navigate:

1. Double-click in the Location Bar, or press `Ctrl+L`, to highlight the URL that is already there.
2. Enter the URL of the page you want to visit. The URL you type replaces any text already in the Location Bar.
3. Press `Enter`.

If you don't know the URL that you need, type a search term into the Search Bar to the right of the Location bar. Your preferred search engine—Google by default—will return a list of websites for you to choose from. (You can also enter your query directly into the Location Bar).

Selecting a link

Most web pages contain links that you can select. These are known as "hyperlinks." A hyperlink can let you move to another page, download a document, change the content of the page, and more.

To select a link:

1. Move the mouse pointer until it changes to a pointing finger. This happens whenever the pointer is over a link. Most links are underlined text, but buttons and pictures on a web page can also be links.
2. Click the link once. While Firefox locates the link's page, status messages will appear at the bottom of the window.

Retracing your steps

If you want to visit a page you have viewed before, there are several ways to do so.

To go backwards and forwards you can also use `Alt+Left` and `Alt+Right` respectively.

- To go back or forward one page, press the **Back** or **Forward** button by the left side of the Location Bar.
- To go back or forward more than one page, click-and-hold on the respective button. You will see a list of pages you have recently visited. To return to a page, select it from the list.
- To see a list of any URLs you have entered into the Location Bar, press the down arrow at the right end of the Location Bar. Choose a page from the list.
- To choose from pages you have visited during the current session, open the **History** menu and choose from the list in the lower section of the menu.
- To choose from pages you have visited over the past few months, open the **History ▸ Show All History** (or press `Ctrl+Shift+H`). Firefox opens a "Library" window showing a list of folders, the first of which is "History." Select a suitable sub-folder, or enter a search term in the search bar (at the top right), to find pages you have viewed before. Double-click a result to open the page.

Stopping and reloading

If a page is loading too slowly or you no longer wish to view a page, press `Esc` to cancel it. To reload the current page if it might have changed since you loaded it, press on the **Reload** button or press `Ctrl+R`.

The **Reload** button is at the right end of the Location Bar.

Opening new windows

At times, you may want to have more than one browser window open. This may help you to organize your browsing session better, or to separate web pages that you are viewing for different reasons.

There are four ways to create a new window:

- On the top bar, select **File ▸ New Window**.
- Press `Ctrl+N`.
- Right-click on Firefox's icon on the Launcher and select **Open New Window**.
- Click on Firefox's icon on the Launcher using your middle mouse button.

Once a new window has opened, you can use it exactly the same as the first window—including navigation and opening tabs. You can open multiple windows.

Opening a link in a new window

Sometimes, you may want to click a link to navigate to another web page, but do not want the original to close. To do this, you can open the link in its own independent window.

There are two ways to open a link in its own window:

- Right-click a link and select **Open Link in New Window**.
- Press-and-hold the `Shift` key while clicking a link.

Tabbed browsing

An alternative to opening new windows is to use *Tabbed Browsing* instead.

Tabbed browsing lets you open several web pages within a single Firefox window, each independent of the other. This frees space on your desktop as you do not have to open a separate window for each new web page. You can open, close, and reload web pages in one place without having to switch to another window.

You can alternate quickly between different tabs by using the keyboard shortcut `Ctrl+Tab`.

> A new tab is independent of other tabs in the same way that new windows are independent of other windows. You can even mix-and-match—for example, one window may contain tabs for your emails, while another window has tabs for your work.

Opening a new blank tab

There are three ways to create a new blank tab:

- Click on the **Open new tab** button (a green plus-sign) on the right side of the last tab.
- On the top bar, open **File ▸ New Tab**.
- Press `Ctrl+T`.

When you create a new tab, it contains a blank page with the Location Bar focused. Type a web address (URL) or other search term to open a website in the new tab.

Opening a link in its own tab

Sometimes, you may want to click a link to navigate to another web page, but do not want the original to close. To do this, you can open the link in its own tab.

There are several ways to open a link in its own tab.

> A tab always opens "in the background"—in other words, the focus remains on the original tab. The last method (`Ctrl+Shift`) is an exception; it focuses the new tab immediately.

- Right-click a link and select **Open Link in New Tab**.
- Press-and-hold the `Ctrl` key while clicking a link.
- Click the link using either the middle mouse button or both left and right mouse buttons simultaneously.
- Drag the link to a blank space on the tab bar or onto the **Open new tab** button.
- Press-and-hold `Ctrl+Shift` while clicking a link.

Closing a tab

Once you have finished viewing a web page in a tab, you have various ways to close it:

- Click on the **Close** button on the right side of the tab.
- Click the tab with the middle mouse button or the mouse wheel.
- Press `Ctrl+W`.
- Right-click the tab and select **Close Tab**.

Restoring a closed tab

Sometimes, you may close the wrong tab by accident, or want to bring back a tab that you have recently closed. Bring back a tab in one of the following two ways:

- Press `Ctrl+Shift+T` to re-open the most recently closed tab.
- Select **History ▸ Recently Closed Tabs**, and choose the name of the tab to restore.

Changing the tab order

Move a tab to a different location on the tab bar by dragging it to a new location using your mouse. While you are dragging the tab, Firefox displays a small indicator to show the tab's new location.

Moving a tab between windows

You can move a tab into a new Firefox window or, if one is already open, into a different Firefox window.

Drag a tab away from the tab bar, and it will open into a new window. Drag it from the tab bar into the tab bar of another open Firefox window, and it will move there instead.

Searching

You can search the web from within Firefox without first visiting the home page of the search engine. By default, Firefox will search the web using the Google search engine.

Searching the web

To search the web in Firefox, type a few words into the Firefox search Bar. For example, if you want to find information about the *Ubuntu*:

1. Move your cursor to the **Search Bar** using your mouse or press `Ctrl+K`.
2. Type the phrase **Ubuntu**. Your typing replaces any text currently in the Search Bar.

3. Press the magnifying glass or `Enter` to search.

Search results from Google for "Ubuntu" will appear in the Firefox window.

Selecting search engines

If you do not want to use Google as your search engine in the Search Bar, you can change the search engine that Firefox uses.

To change your preferred search engine, press the search logo (at the left of your Search Bar—Google by default) and choose the search engine of your choice. Some search engines, such as Bing, Google and Yahoo, search the whole web; others, such as Amazon and Wikipedia, search only specific sites.

Figure 3.8: These are the other search engines you can use—by default—from the Firefox search bar.

Searching the web for words selected in a web page

Sometimes, you may want to search for a phrase that you see on a web page. You can copy and paste the phrase into the Search Bar, but there is a quicker way.

1. Highlight the word or phrase in a web page using your left mouse button.
2. Right-click the highlighted text and select **Search [Search Engine] for [your selected words]**.

Firefox passes the highlighted text to the search engine, and opens a new tab with the results.

Searching within a page

Figure 3.9: You can search within web pages using the **Find Toolbar**.

You may want to look for specific text within the web page you are viewing. To find text within the current page in Firefox:

1. Choose **Edit ▸ Find** or press `Ctrl+F` to open the **Find Toolbar** at the bottom of Firefox.
2. Enter your search query into the **Find** field in the Find Toolbar. The search automatically begins as soon as you type something into the field.
3. Once some text has been matched on the web page, you can:
   - Click on **Next** to find text in the page that is below the current cursor position.
   - Click on **Previous** to find text that is above the current cursor position.
   - Click on **Highlight all** to highlight all occurrences of your search words in the current page.
   - Select the **Match case** option to limit the search to text that has the same capitalization as your search words.

To quickly find the same word or phrase again, press `F3`.
You can skip opening the **Find Toolbar** altogether.

1. Turn on the relevant Accessibility option with **Edit ▸ Preferences ▸ Advanced ▸ General ▸ Accessibility ▸ Search for text when I start typing ▸ Close**.
2. Now, provided your cursor is not within a text field, when you start typing, it will automatically start searching for text.

Viewing web pages full screen

To display more web content on the screen, you can use *Full Screen mode*. Full Screen mode hides everything but the main content. To enable Full Screen mode, choose **View ▸ Full Screen** or press F11. While in full-screen mode, move your mouse to the top of the screen to reveal the URL and search bars.

Press F11 to return to normal mode.

Copying and saving pages

With Firefox, you can copy part of a page so that you can paste it elsewhere, or save the page or part of a page as a file on your computer.

Copying part of a page

To copy text, links or images from a page:

1. Highlight the text and images with your mouse.
2. Right-click the highlighted text and select **Copy**, or press Ctrl+C.

To copy just a single image, it is not necessary to highlight it. Just right-click the image and select **Copy**.

You can paste the results into another application, such as LibreOffice.

Copying a link

To copy a text or image link (URL) from a page:

1. Position the pointer over the text, link or image. Your mouse pointer changes to a pointing finger.
2. Right-click the link or image to open a pop-up menu.
3. Select **Copy Link Location**.

You can paste the link into other applications or into Firefox's Location Bar.

Saving all or part of a page

To save an entire page in Firefox:

1. Choose **File ▸ Save Page As** from the top bar, or press Ctrl+S. Firefox opens the "Save As" window.
2. Choose a location for the saved page.
3. Type a file name for the page.
4. Press **Save**.

To save an image from a page:

1. Position the mouse pointer over the image.

2. Right-click the image and select **Save Image As**. Firefox opens the "Save Image" window.
3. Choose a location for the saved image.
4. Enter a file name for the image.
5. Press **Save**.

Changing your home page

Firefox shows the *home page* when it opens. By default, this is the Ubuntu Start Page. You can change your default home page to a new one, or even to several new ones.

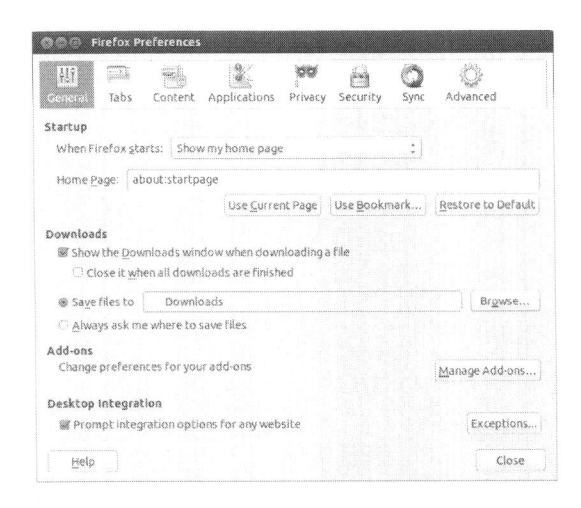

Figure 3.10: Change Firefox settings in this window.

To change your home page:

1. Navigate to the page that you would like to become your new home page. If you want Firefox to open more than one tab when it starts, open a new tab and navigate to the extra page as many times as you would like.
2. Choose **Edit ▸ Preferences ▸ General ▸ Startup ▸ Use Current Pages ▸ Close**.

The home page can also be set by entering the addresses that should be open in the **Home Page**, with a pipe ("|") separating pages to be opened in separate tabs.

Download settings

In **Edit ▸ Preferences ▸ General ▸ Downloads**, you can hide or show the Downloads window, tell Firefox where to place downloaded files, and whether or not to ask where each time.

The *Downloads* window shows the progress of currently downloading files, and lists files downloaded in the past. It can be used to open or re-download files.

Bookmarks

When browsing the web you may want to come back to certain web pages again without having to remember the URL. To do this, you *bookmark* each page. These bookmarks are saved in the web browser, and you can use them to re-open to those web pages.

Bookmarking a page

After navigating to a web page you can save its location by bookmarking it. There are two ways to bookmark a page:

- From the top bar, choose **Bookmarks ▸ Bookmark This Page**, or press `Ctrl+D`. A window opens, allowing you to provide a descriptive name for the bookmark and a location (within the browser's bookmarks) to save it. Press **Done** to save.
- Press the *star* on the right-hand side in the Location Bar. It turns yellow. This saves the page in the *Unsorted Bookmarks* folder.

Navigating to a bookmarked page

To navigate to a bookmarked page, open the **Bookmarks** menu from the top bar, and choose your bookmark. Firefox opens the bookmark in the current tab.

> *You can reveal the bookmarks, including the Unsorted Bookmarks, in a sidebar on the left of the browser window. Select **View ▸ Sidebar ▸ Bookmarks**, or press* `Ctrl+B`. *Repeat, or press the **close button** at its top, to hide the sidebar.*

Deleting or editing a bookmark

To delete or edit a bookmark, do one of the following:

- If you are viewing the page already, the star in the Location Bar will be yellow. Press it. Firefox opens a small pop-up window, where you can either **Remove Bookmark** or edit the bookmark.
- Select **Bookmarks ▸ Show All Bookmarks** or press `Shift+Ctrl+O`. In the window that opens, you can navigate to bookmarks. Select the one you would like to change. To delete, right-click and choose **Delete** or press `Delete` on your keyboard. To edit, change the details shown at the bottom of the window.

History

Whenever you are browsing the web, Firefox saves your browsing history. This allows you to come back to a web page that you have recently visited without needing to remember or bookmark the page's URL.

To see your most recent history, open the **History** menu from the top bar. The menu displays several of the most recent web pages that you have viewed. Choose one of the pages to return to it.

To view the complete history, either:

- Select **View ▸ History** or press `Ctrl+H` to view the history in a sidebar; this replaces the bookmarks sidebar if it is open. (Repeat, or press the **close button** at its top, to hide the sidebar.)
- Select **History ▸ Show All History** or press `Shift+Ctrl+H` to view the history in a pop-up window.

Your browsing history is categorized as "Today," "Yesterday," "Last 7 days," "This month," the previous five months by name, and finally "Older than 6 months." If history for a category does not exist, that category will not be listed. Select one of the date categories in the sidebar to expand it and reveal the pages that you visited during that time. Once you find the page you want, select it to re-display it.

You can also search for a page by its title or URL. Enter a few letters from one or more words or, optionally, the URL in the **Search** field at the top of the history sidebar. The sidebar displays a list of web pages matching your search words. Select the page you want. (You can even do this in the Location Bar, saving you from having to open the History sidebar or pop-up window.)

Clearing private data

Firefox stores all its data only on your computer. Nevertheless, if you share your computer, you may at times want to delete all private data.

Select **Tools ▸ Clear Recent History** or press `Shift+Ctrl+Delete`. Choose your **Time range to clear**, and under **Details** which items to clear, and press **Clear Now**.

Preventing Firefox from recording private data

You can start "private browsing," where Firefox will not record anything permanently. This lasts until you turn it off or until you restart Firefox.

Choose **Tools ▸ Start Private Browsing** or press `Shift+Ctrl+P`. Press the button **Start Private Browsing** to confirm. As long as you remain in this mode, Firefox will not record browsing, download, form or search history, or cookies, nor will it cache files. However, if you bookmark anything or download files, these will be retained.

Repeat **Tools ▸ Start Private Browsing** or `Shift+Ctrl+P`, or restart Firefox, to end private browsing.

Using a different web browser

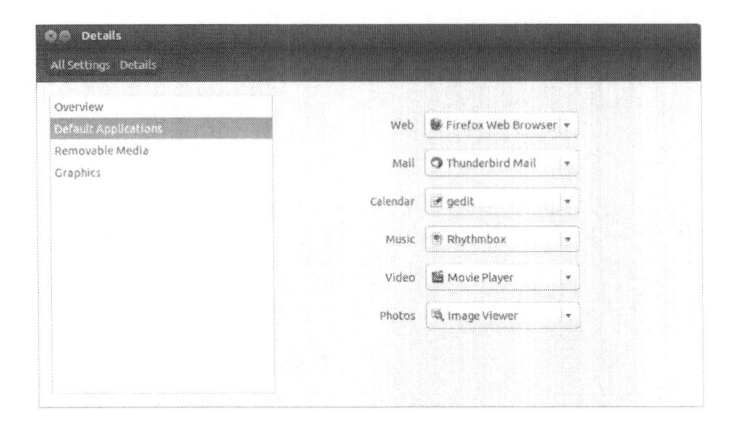

Figure 3.11: The Default Applications where you can change your preferred browser.

If you choose to install a different web browser on your computer, you may want to use it as the default browser when you click links from emails, instant messages, and other places. Canonical supports Firefox and Chromium (Google's Linux version of Chrome), but there are several others that you can install.

To change your preferred web browser, open **Session Indicator** from the top panel on the far right-hand side, and open **System Settings ▸ Details ▸ Default Applications**. Choose your preferred web browser from the drop-down menu **Web**.

Reading and composing email

Introduction to Thunderbird

Thunderbird is an email client developed by Mozilla and is easy to setup and use. It is free, fast, and comes packed full of useful features. Even if you are new to Ubuntu and Thunderbird, you will be up and running in no time, checking your email and staying in touch with friends and family.

Setting up Thunderbird

In the top right corner of the Ubuntu desktop you will see an envelope icon in the notification area. This is the *messaging menu*. From here, you can launch Thunderbird by clicking **set up mail**. Alternatively, you can click the Ubuntu button in the top left corner of the screen at the top of the Launcher to bring up the Dash and type `thunderbird` into the search box. Once Thunderbird opens, you will be greeted by a pop-up box prompting you to setup your email account.

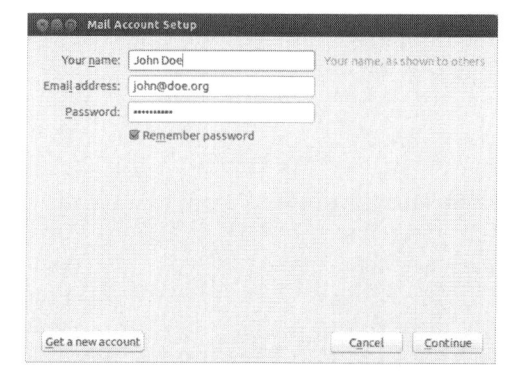

Figure 3.12: Setting up Thunderbird

Before a valid email account is set up in Thunderbird, the first screen to appear will be an introductory message from Mozilla inviting you to set up an email account through a local service provider in your area. For the purposes of these instructions, we will assume you already have an email address, so you can click on the button in the lower right corner of the screen that says **Skip this and use my existing email**.

On the next screen titled **Mail account setup**, enter your name in the first text box, your email address in the second text box (for example, username@domain.com), and your email password in the third text box.

Once completed, click the **continue** button. Thunderbird will automatically set up your email account for you. When Thunderbird finishes detecting your email settings, click **create account** and Thunderbird will do the rest. You can also set Thunderbird as your default news and RSS reader by checking the boxes in the pop-up box that appear after you click create your account. If you don't want to see this message box every time you start Thunderbird, simply deselect **Always perform this check when starting Thunderbird**. You are now ready to start using Thunderbird.

Around the Thunderbird workspace

Now that you have your email account set up, let's get to know the Thunderbird workspace. Thunderbird is designed to be very user-friendly and easy to navigate. When you open the application, you will see the main workspace with your email folders (all folders window) on the left. On the right of the screen, you will see two windows. The top-right window displays a list of your received email, and the bottom-right window displays the current email you are viewing. The size of these windows can be easily resized to suit your viewing environment. To resize the windows, simply left-click and hold the dividing bar that separates the two windows and drag the bar up or down to the desired position. The *All Folders* window is where you can see your mail folders. This window can also include:

Inbox Where your email is stored and accessed
Email address folder You will see one of these folders for each of the accounts you have setup
Drafts Where your draft emails are stored
Sent mail Where the emails you have sent are stored
Spam This is where suspected spam email is stored so you can check them to make sure you haven't lost any important emails
Trash This is where messages you've deleted are stored so you can double check to make sure you haven't accidentally deleted an important email (also one of the local folders)
Important This is where emails you have marked as important are stored
Starred This is where emails you have marked with a star are stored
Personal This is where emails you have marked as personal are stored
Receipts You can move important receipts to this folder.
Travel You can use this folder to store travel emails such as flight times and bookings
Work You can store work emails in this folder to keep them separate from your personal email
Outbox Where the emails you are in the process of sending are stored (also one of the local folders)

Across the top of the Thunderbird workspace, you will see four control buttons, **get mail**, **write**, **address book**, and **tag**. These are used to get your mail, write your mail, access your address book, and tag your email messages.

At the top-right of the *All Folders* window, you will see a set of quick filter buttons, **unread**, **starred**, **contact**, **tags**, and**attachment**. You can use these buttons to filter your email messages so that you only see your unread mail, your favorite mail (starred), mail from people in your address book, mail you have tagged, and mail that includes attachments.

If you are accustomed to a more traditional desktop and you have Thunderbird maximized to full screen, you might be wondering where the menus are located. They are still there, and if you want to access them, move your mouse to the top of the screen and you will see the familiar menus: **file**, **edit**, **view**, **go**, **message**, **tools**, and **help**.

At the top of the window that displays your email, you can see six action buttons, **reply**, **reply all**, **forward**, **archive**, **junk**, and **delete**. You will find these very useful for quickly replying to email, forwarding your email to another person, archiving (backing up) your email, marking an email as junk mail, and quickly deleting an email. To the left of these quick action buttons, you will see information about the email you are viewing that includes the sender's name, the subject of the email, the reply address, and the recipient of the email.

Using your address book

At the top of the main workspace, you will see the **address book** button. Click this button to access your address book. Once the address book opens you, will see the address book window. From here, you can easily organize your contacts. At the top of the address book window, you will see five buttons, **new contact**, **new list**, **properties**, **write**, and **delete**. They function in the following ways:

New Contact This button allows you to add a new contact and add as much detail as you wish to save, including name, nickname, address, email, additional email, screen name, work number, home number, fax, pager and mobile/cell number.

New List This button allows you to add lists for your contacts such as family, friends, acquaintances, etc.

Properties This button allows you to rename your address book name. The default name is *personal address book*, but you can change the name as you see fit.

Write This button allows you to quickly send an email to a selected contact without needing to go back to the main Thunderbird workspace. Simply select a contact from your contacts list and click the **write** button to send them an email.

Delete This button allows you to quickly delete a contact from your address book. Just select the contact you want to delete and press **delete** to remove the contact from your address book.

Checking and reading messages

Thunderbird will automatically check your email account for new messages every ten minutes, but if you need to manually check for new messages at any time, left-click the **get mail button** in the top left corner of the workspace. Thunderbird will then check your email account for new messages and download them. As they are downloaded, you will see the new email appear in the message window on the right side of the workspace. When you click on one of your emails, it will appear in the window below your email list. If you want to view your email in a full window, double-left-click your chosen email, and Thunderbird will display the email in a full window in its own tab. At the top of the open email, you will see information about the email and the five quick action buttons, **reply**, **forward**, **archive**, **junk** and **delete** as previously discussed. If an email has remote content, you will see a message asking if you want to display the email or not. You may want to filter your emails from time to time; this is easily done with Thunderbird. When you have an email selected and you want to tag the email, simply click the **tag** button and a drop-down list will be displayed. In this drop-down list, you have the options to **Remove All Tags** or **Mark as...**, **Important**, **Work**, **Personal**, **To Do**, **Later**. You can also **create a new tag** more suited to your own personal requirements.

Remote content represent parts of an email that may be hosted elsewhere. Remote content might consist of video or audio, but most often is graphics or HTML content. For security purposes, Thunderbird will as you if you wish to view this remote content.

Composing and Replying to Messages

To compose a new email message, click the **write** button in the top left of the workspace. This will bring up a new window where you can compose your new email. In the **To:** field, enter the email address of the destination —the contact to whom you are sending this email. If there is more than one contact to whom you are writing, separate multiple recipients with commas.

If a contact that you are addressing is in your address book, you can address them by name. Start typing the name of the contact; Thunderbird will display the list of mailing contacts below your text. Once you see the contact you intend to address, click on their email address or use the down arrow key and then press **Enter** to select the address. If you would like to carbon-copy (Cc) some contacts, click the **To:** field and select **Cc:**. Contacts who are listed on the **To:** and **Cc:** lines will receive the email, and will see the rest of the contacts to whom an email was sent. If you would like to send an email to some contacts without disclosing to whom your email was sent, you can send a blind carbon-copy, or **Bcc**. To enable **Bcc**, select **Bcc:** by clicking the **To:** field and selecting **Bcc:**. Any contacts entered in the **Bcc:** field will receive the message, but none of the recipients will see the names or emails of contacts on the **Bcc:** line. Instead of typing the email addresses or names of the contacts you are addressing in the message, you can select the contacts from your address book. Start typing a few letters from your contact's first or last name in the **To:** field to filter the list to only show mailing contacts. Once you identify the contact you would like to address, click on their name in the list. If you've added the contact in error, delete their address and enter the correct address. You may enter a subject for your email in the *Subject* field. Messages should have a subject to help the recipient identify the general contents of the email while glancing at their message list. Enter the contents of your message in the big text field below the subject. There is no practical limit on the amount of text you can include in your message. By default, Thunderbird will auto-detect the correct format for your email but you can change this by clicking **Options** then mouse over **Format** and select your preferred option from the list. You have a choice of *Auto-Detect, Plain Text Only, Rich Text (HTML) Only,* and *Plain and Rich (HTML) Text.* When you have finished composing your email, click on the **Send** button on the window's toolbar. Your message will be placed in the Outbox, and will be sent to your desired recipient.

> If you do not include a subject in your email, Thunderbird will warn you about this omission.

Attaching files

At times, you may want to send files to your contacts. To send files, you will need to attach them to your email message. To attach a file to an email you are composing, click on the **Attach** button. When the new window opens, select the file you want to send and click **open**. The file you selected will then be attached to the email when you click send.

> You can attach quite a few different file types to emails, but be careful about the size of the attachments! If they are too big, some email systems will reject the email you are sending, and your recipient will never receive it!

Replying to Messages

In addition to composing new messages, you may want to reply to messages that you receive. There are three types of email replies:

Reply or *Reply to Sender* sends your reply only to the sender of the message to whom you are replying.
Reply to All sends your reply to the sender of the message as well as any address in **To:** or **Cc:** lines.
Forward allows you to send the message, with any additional comments you may add, to some other contacts.

To use any of these methods, click on the message to which you want to reply and then click the **Reply**, **Reply to All**, or **Forward** button on the message toolbar. Thunderbird will open the reply window. This window should look much like the window for composing new messages, but the

To:, Cc:, **Subject:**, and main message content fields should be filled in from the message to which you are replying. Edit the **To:**, **Cc:**, **Bcc:**, **Subject:** or main body as you see fit. When your reply is finished, click on the **Send** button on the toolbar. Your message will be placed in the *Outbox* and will be sent.

Using instant messaging

Instant messaging allows you to communicate with people in real time online. Ubuntu includes the Empathy application that lets you use instant messaging features to keep in touch with your contacts. To start Empathy, open the **Messaging Menu** (the envelope icon on the menu bar), then select **Chat**.

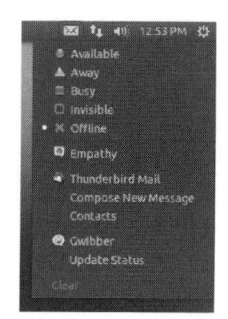

Figure 3.13: This is the icon that Empathy displays in the launcher.

Figure 3.14: Access Empathy from the Messaging Menu in the menu bar.

Empathy lets you connect to many instant messaging networks. You can connect to: Google Accounts, Windows Live, Salut, Yahoo!, Jabber, and AIM.

Running Empathy for the first time

When you open Empathy for the first time, you should see a screen similar to that in figure 3.15. At this time, Empathy does not know about any of your instant messaging accounts.

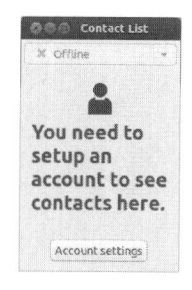

Figure 3.15: You should see a window like this the first time you open Empathy.

Adding accounts

⚠ *You must have existing chat accounts to that are compatible with Empathy. If you do not have an existing account, you will need to create one before continuing.*

You can add accounts to be used with empathy by clicking the **Account Settings** button, as shown in figure 3.15, or you can use the menu bar to navigate to **Empathy ▸ Accounts**. You should see a dialog similar to that in figure 3.16. This is the Online Accounts manager.

Be aware that when you Add or Remove accounts using the Online Accounts manager you will be adding or removing those accounts to or from *all* the applications that they integrate with, not just Empathy.

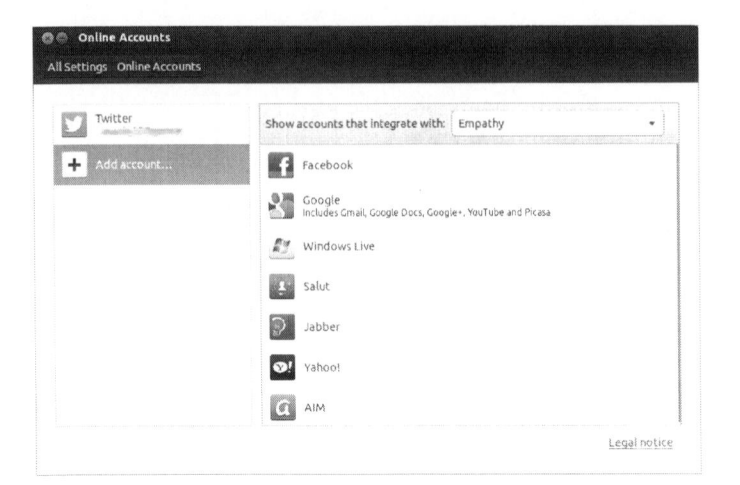

Figure 3.16: Add your existing chat accounts for use in Empathy using the Online Accounts manager.

Click **Add account...** on the left-hand side of the window if it is not already selected. At the top of the window, where it says *Show accounts that integrate with:*, select *Empathy* from the drop-down menu. Now click on the name of the chat service with which you have an account. Shown in figure 3.17, we have selected a Google account. You must now enter your login credentials and authorize Empathy to access your account.

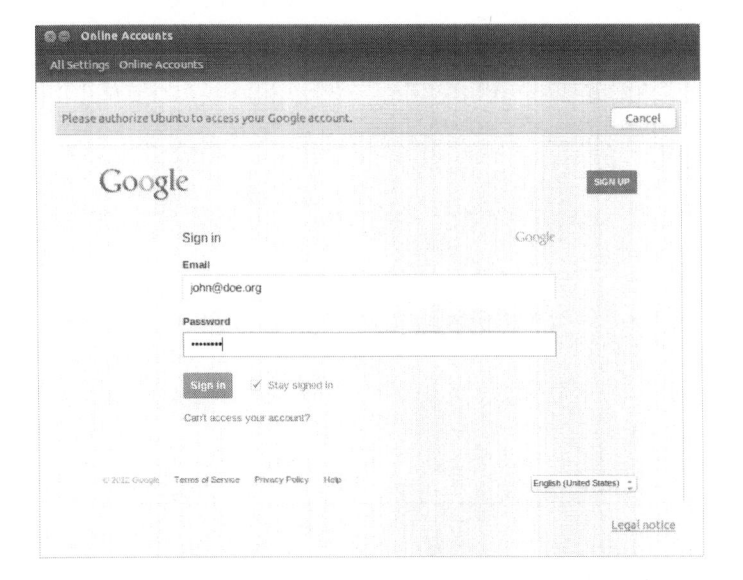

Figure 3.17: You must enter your account credentials and authorize Empathy to use your account.

After adding your accounts, you can now use Empathy to chat with all of your friends, right from your Ubuntu desktop!

Communicating with contacts

Text

To communicate with a contact, select the contact in Empathy's main window and double-click their name. Empathy should open a new window where you can type messages to your contact and see a record of previously exchanged messages.

To send a message to the contact, enter your message in the text field below the conversation history. When you have typed your message press

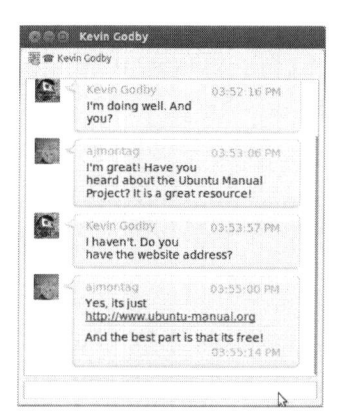

Figure 3.18: Chatting with friends in Empathy.

the Enter key to send the message to your contact. When the person you are chatting with is typing to you, a small keyboard icon will appear next to their name in the chat window.

If you are communicating with more than one person, then all of the conversations will be shown in tabs in your Empathy window.

Audio and Video Calling

You can use Empathy to chat with your friends using audio and video, too. To start an audio or video call, right click on the Contact name, then select **Audio Call** or **Video Call**, as shown in figure 3.19. This will notify the person you are trying to call, and they will be asked if they would like to answer the call.

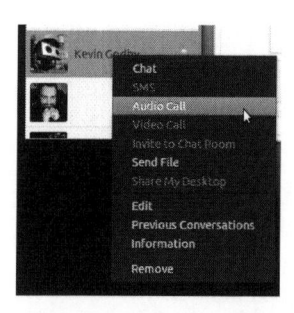

Figure 3.19: Right-clicking a contact exposes many ways to communicate.

If the person you are calling accepts your call request, you will be connected, and you can begin talking. If the person you are calling cannot see or hear you, your webcam or microphone may not be properly configured; see the sections on Sound and Using a webcam, respectively. You can end the call by clicking on the red telephone button in the chat window.

Sending and receiving files

Sending a file

When you are in a conversation with a contact and you would like to send them a file, right-click the contact in the contact list—as in figure 3.19— and select **Send File**. Empathy should open the "Select file" window. Find the file you wish to send, and click on the **Send** button. A "File Transfers" window will open showing the file and its transfer progress. When the file transfer is complete, you can close the "File Transfers" window.

Changing your status

You can use your status to show your contacts how busy you are or what you are doing. Your contacts see your status next to your name when they chat with you. You can use the standard statuses, which are:

- Available
- Away
- Busy
- Invisible
- Offline

Two of these statuses have additional functionality. The *Invisible* status lets you see which of your contacts are online, but does not allow them to see that you are online. The *Offline* status logs you out entirely; you will not be able to see which of your contacts are online, nor can they see you or chat with you.

You can change your status in one of two ways. The first method is in the main Empathy window from the drop-down list at the top of the window.

The same drop-down list lets you set a custom status by choosing "Custom Message..." next to the icon that matches your status. Enter what you would like your status to say, and click on the green check mark.

The second method is to click the **Messaging Icon** on the menu bar, as shown in figure 3.14. From this menu, you will see all of the same options that Empathy presents, but accessible without having to open Empathy.

Desktop Sharing

Desktop sharing is a very nice feature available with Ubuntu. It can be used for a lot of purposes, like troubleshooting, online meetings, or just showing off your cool desktop to your friend. It is very easy to get remote desktop sharing working between two Ubuntu machines.

To share your screen, you will first have to set up Desktop Sharing. Open the Desktop Sharing application from the Launcher. Next, select **Allow other users to view your desktop**; you may want to deselect **Allow other users to control your desktop**.

After you have Desktop Sharing configured, open Empathy. To begin sharing your desktop, right-click on the contact you wish to share with, and select **Share my desktop**.

It should be noted that the other user will obviously be able to see the information displayed on your screen. Please be sure to keep this in mind if you have documents or files that are of a private nature open on your desktop.

Changing account settings

If you need to add more accounts after the initial launch of Empathy, open the **Edit** menu, then select **Accounts**. Empathy will then display the Online Accounts manager window.

Editing an account

You might need to edit the details of an account. Select the account you want to change on the left side of the Online Accounts window then click

Options. The Online Accounts manager should show the current information for the account. Once you have made your changes, click **Done**.

Removing an account

To remove an account select the account on the left hand side of the window and click on the **Remove account** button. The Online Accounts manager should open the "Are you sure you wish to remove this Ubuntu Web Account" window. Click on the **Remove** button to confirm that you want to remove the account, or click **Cancel** to keep the account.

Be aware that when you Add or Remove accounts using the Online Accounts manager you will be adding or removing those accounts to or from *all* the applications that they integrate with, not just Empathy.

Editing contacts

Adding a contact

To add a contact open the **Chat** menu, then select **Add contact**. Empathy should open the "New Contact" window.

In the **Account** drop-down list, choose the account you want to add contact information. When creating a contact you must select the service that matches the service your contact is using.

For example, if your contact's address ends in "@googlemail.com" then you will need to add it to an account that ends in "@googlemail.com." Likewise if the contact's email ends in "@hotmail.com" then you will need to add it to an account ending in "@hotmail.com."

After choosing the account you wish to add the contact to, enter their login ID, their username, their screen name, or their email address in the **Identifier** text field. Next, in the **Alias** text field, enter the name you want to see in your contact list. Click **Add** to add the contact to your list of contacts.

Removing a contact

Click on the contact that you want to remove, then on the Unity bar at the top of the screen, open the **Edit** menu, select **Contact**, then **Remove**. This will open the "Remove contact" window.

Click on the **Remove** button to confirm that you want to remove this contact, or click **Cancel** to keep the contact.

Microblogging

Gwibber is the default microblogging application that lets you access multiple social networking accounts, without having to open an Internet browser. Gwibber can be used to access and post on Twitter, Facebook, Identi.ca, Ping.fm, Flickr, Digg, Status.net, Foursquare, Qaiku and Friend-Feed.

Upgrades and add-ons

If you need add-ons for Ping.fm, Flickr, Digg, Status.net, Foursquare, Qaiku and FriendFeed you need to install them before you begin using Gwibber. Go to the Ubuntu Software Center and search for Gwibber. Click on Gwibber and press **More Info** to get the window shown in figure 3.20. Check each add-on that you want (or just select all of them), and press **Apply Changes**. Wait for them to finish installing. You need to log out and in again to activate the add-ons.

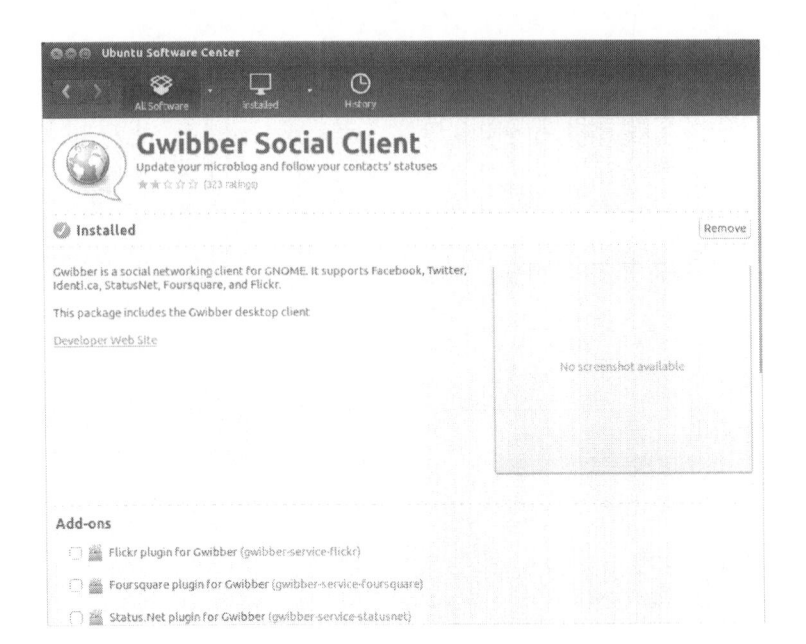

Figure 3.20: Use the Ubuntu Software Center to to get Gwibber add-ons.

Working with social networking accounts on Gwibber

Pull down the Message menu from the top panel bar as shown in figure 3.21 and select **Gwibber**. This starts the app.

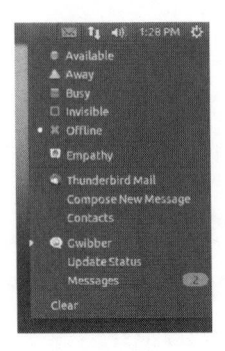

Figure 3.21: The Message pull-down menu shows you a quick overview of your feeds.

If you have not previously entered an account, the Online Accounts manager will open automatically. Otherwise, select **Edit ▸ Accounts** to open it.

Figure 3.22: Add an account for use with Gwibber using the Online Accounts manager.

To add a new account, click +. At the top of the window, where it says *Show accounts that integrate with:*, select *Gwibber* from the drop-down menu. Now click on the name of the service with which you have an account and follow any instructions to authorize the account.

Removing accounts from Gwibber is easy too. Go to the Online Accounts manager window and select the account to be removed. Click the **Remove account** button to remove the account.

> You can add more than one account from a service provider.

> Be aware that when you Add or Remove accounts using the Online Accounts manager you will be adding or removing those accounts to or from *all* the applications that they integrate with, not just Gwibber.

Using Gwibber to follow streams

Gwibber displays feeds from each service provider as *streams*. You can list them in either ascending or descending order by selecting **View ▸ Sort**. You can separate the feeds as messages, replies, and private messages. In addition the attachments from the feed are sorted as images, links and videos. Click the image, link or video to take you to the website in a new tab in your default browser. Images can be previewed within Gwibber.

Figure 3.23: A stream in Gwibber. Clicking on the image should open the Facebook page in a browser.

Notifications

You can customize how feeds display in the notification bubble, and the frequency with which Gwibber refreshes, in the preferences (**Edit ▸ Preferences**).

Figure 3.24: A notification from Gwibber. Notifications can be customized from the Gwibber Preferences menu.

Replying, Liking and Retweeting

Each post can be liked, retweeted or replied to, from within Gwibber's window, by clicking on the feed's icon at the top right of each post. This displays a menu of the actions available for that feed. Figure 3.25 shows the menu for the Twitter feed..

Figure 3.25: You can similarly "like" or comment on updates from within Gwibber.

Updating your Status

To update your status using Gwibber, select **Update Status** from the Message icon in the Top Panel; this opens a new window. Type your status message and post it to all your accounts with one click. Press **Esc** to cancel.

You can also shorten URLs as you post from Gwibber using a list of URL shortening services. Play with Gwibber and discover other cool things it can do. Go to http://gwibber.com/docs/user-guide/current/master_social_networking_with_gwibber.pdf for more information.

Viewing and editing photos

Shotwell Photo Manager is the default photo application in Ubuntu. This application allows you to view, tag, edit, and share your photos. To start Shotwell, click on the Dash near the top-left of the screen, then select the Shotwell icon labeled **View Photos**. If you do not see Shotwell, simply type **Shotwell** in the search bar at the top of the Dash, and you will see the Shotwell application soon appear.

Figure 3.26: Manage your photo collection, enhance your photos while keeping the original, and share your memories online using Shotwell Photo Manager.

Importing Photos

When you launch Shotwell for the first time, you will be greeted by the "Welcome!" window which gives you instructions on how to import photos. Click **OK**. You can now import photos by dragging the photos into the Shotwell window or by connecting your camera or external storage device to the computer.

From a digital camera   Connect your camera to the computer using the data cable, and turn on the power to your camera. If your camera is properly detected, you will see a new window prompting you to launch an application. Select **Shotwell** in the drop-down menu then click **OK**. Your camera will be listed in the Shotwell sidebar. Select your camera in the sidebar. You will see a preview of the camera's contents. Select individual photos by pressing and holding Ctrl and clicking on each photo you want to import, and then click **Import Selected** on the bottom bar of the window. Or, you can choose to import all photos by clicking **Import All**.

From your computer   You can import photos into Shotwell by dragging photos from your file browser into the Shotwell window. Alternatively, you can click **File Import From Folder,** ‣ select the folder containing the photos you want to import.

From external hard drive, usb flash drive, or cd/dvd   Importing photos from external storage is similar to importing from your computer. Your external storage device may also appear under the **Camera** label on the Shotwell sidebar. Follow the instructions for importing from a camera or computer.

Choosing where Shotwell saves photos

The default location for the Shotwell Library is your `Pictures` folder in your home directory. When importing pictures using the "Import" window, you will be given the option to copy the files to your Library, or keep the files in place.

If you have your photos stored on your computer, the option **Import in Place** will be suitable. This will prevent photos from being duplicated. If you are importing photos from an external source, such as a portable hard drive, usb flash drive, or cd/dvd, you should select **Copy into Library** so the photos are copied to your computer—otherwise they won't appear when you remove the external source.

Viewing photos

Choose **Library** or any collection in the sidebar to display photos from your selection. Use the slider on the bottom bar to adjust the size of the thumbnails. To view a full-window image, double-click an individual photo. In the full-window view, you can navigate through the collection using the backward and forward arrows, zoom in on the image using the slider, pan by clicking and dragging the image, and exit the full-window view by double-clicking the image.

To view the collection in full-screen mode, press F11 or go to **View ‣ Fullscreen**. You can navigate through the collection using the toolbar by moving your mouse to the bottom of the screen. To view a slideshow presentation of the collection, press F5 or go to **View ▸ Slideshow**. Press the Esc key to exit the *Fullscreen* or *Slideshow* views.

Organizing photos

Shotwell makes finding photos of the same type easier by using *tags*. You can apply as many tags to a photo as you like. To apply tags to photos, first select the photos. Then right-click on the photos and select **Add Tags**. Enter the tags you want into the text field, separated by commas. If you are adding new tags, these will appear in the side bar on the right under the **Tags** label.

Editing images

You may want to edit some of the photos you import into Shotwell. For example, you may want to remove something at the edge, adjust the color, reduce the red-eye effect, or straighten the image. To edit a photo, double-click on the photo you want to edit, and then click on one of the following buttons:

Rotate

Click **Rotate** to rotate the image 90° clockwise. You can click the button more than once and it will rotate the image clockwise in 90° intervals.

Crop

Click **Crop** to change the framing of the photo. The image will darken and a selection will appear. Adjust the selection to your desired crop by dragging a corner or side. If you want to choose a specific aspect ratio, use the drop-down menu to select one of the preset ratios or enter your own custom ratio. A pivot button is provided to change your selection from landscape to portrait and vice versa. Once you are happy with the selection, click **OK** to apply the crop or **Cancel** to discard it.

Red-eye reduction

If you have taken a photo and the flash has caused the subject to have red eyes, you can fix this problem in Shotwell.
  Click the **Red-eye** button. A circle will appear.
  Drag this circle over one of the subjects eyes and then use the slider to adjust the circle size.
  When the circle is over the eye, click **Apply** to fix the red eye. You will need to repeat this for each individual eye. Use caution when adjusting the size of the circle. A circle too large and covering the skin may cause discoloration when applying the red-eye reduction.

Adjust

Clicking **Adjust** will bring up a window that lets you edit a few things:

Level Similar to contrast
Exposure How bright the image is
Saturation How colorful the image is
Tint The overall color

Temperature Whether the image is warm (more yellow) or cool (more blue)
Shadows How dark the shadows are

To change these values, drag the sliders until you are satisfied with the image. Click **OK** to apply the changes, **Reset** to undo the changes and start over, or **Cancel** to discard the changes.

Auto-adjustment with *Enhance*

Click **Enhance** to let Shotwell automatically adjust the color, levels, exposure, contrast, and temperature to create a more pleasing image.

Reverting an edited photo to the original

When you edit a photo in Shotwell, your original image remains untouched. You can undo all of the changes and revert to the original version by right-clicking on the photo, then selecting **Revert to Original**. This option is only available for photos you have edited.

Sharing your photos

You can easily share your photos on the web using Shotwell's Publish feature. Select the photos you want to share, then click the **Publish** button located on the bottom bar. Choose Facebook, Flickr, or Picasa Web Albums in the drop-down menu and log-in with your credentials. Some services may require you to authorize Shotwell before allowing the application to publish photos. Follow the instructions in the window, select your desired options, and click **Publish** to upload your images to the web.

Further information

We've only just touched on the features of Shotwell. To get more help, select **Help ▸ Contents**. This will load the online manual, where you can get more detailed instructions on how to use Shotwell effectively.

Watching videos and movies

To watch videos or DVDs in Ubuntu, you can use the Movie Player application. To start the Movie Player, click on the Dash, then search for "Movie Player" and select it. This will open the "Movie Player" window.

Figure 3.27: Movie player (Totem) plays music and videos.

Codecs

Watching DVDs may require Ubuntu to install a coder-decoder (also known as a "codec"), a piece of software allowing your computer to understand the contents of the DVD and display the video.

⚠ *Legal Notice: Patent and copyright laws differ depending on which country you are in. Please obtain legal advice if you are unsure whether a particular patent or restriction applies to a media format you wish to use in your country.*

So that you can play all videos and DVDs, you will need to install codecs. To install the codecs, open the Ubuntu Software Center either through the Dash or the Launcher. When the "Ubuntu Software Center" window opens, use the search box in the top right and search for the following:

- ubuntu-restricted-extras
- libdvdread4
- libdvdnav4

Double-click each item above and then click the **Install** button. This may open an "Authenticate" window. If so, enter your password, then click **Authenticate** to start the installation process.

Playing videos from file

Open the **Movie** menu, then select **Open**.... This will open the "Select Movies or Playlists" window. Find the file or files that you want to play and click on the **Add** button. The video or videos will start playing.

Playing a DVD

When you insert a DVD in the computer, Ubuntu should open the "You have just inserted a Video DVD. Choose what application to launch" window. Make sure that **Open Movie Player** is chosen in the drop-down list and then click **OK**. The "Movie Player" window will open and the movie will begin.

If the "Movie Player" window is already open, open the **Movie** menu, then select **Play Disc**... and the movie will begin.

Listening to audio and music

Ubuntu comes with the Rhythmbox Music Player for listening to your music, streaming Internet radio and managing playlists and podcasts. Rhythmbox can also help you find and purchase music, along with managing subscriptions to your favorite RSS feeds.

Starting Rhythmbox

There are several ways to start Rhythmbox.

- Open the Dash, select **Listen to Music**, and choose any of the displayed music files (if you have any).
- Open the Dash, type *Rhythmbox* and click on the Rhythmbox Music Player icon.

Figure 3.28: Rhythmbox Music Player

- Ubuntu 12.04 comes with an indicator menu in the top bar for sound-related applications and devices. This menu includes a link to start Rhythmbox, and basic playback and volume controls.

If you close Rhythmbox by pressing Alt+F4 or clicking the red close button (●), it will disappear from view but continue to play in the background. You can still control your music or reopen from the Sound indicator. To quit Rhythmbox completely, press Ctrl+Q or choose **Music ▸ Quit** from the menu bar.

Playing music

To play music, you must first import music into your library. Choose **Music ▸ Import Folder…** or press Ctrl+O on your keyboard to import a folder containing media, a single file, an Amazon MP3 purchase, or media from an iOS or Android device. The Rhythmbox toolbar contains most of the controls that you will use for browsing and playing your music. If you want to play a song, double-click a track; or click it and press the **Play** button on the toolbar, choose **Control ▸ Play** from the menu bar, or press Ctrl+Space. When a song is playing, the **Play** button will become a **Pause** button. Use this button, **Control ▸ Play**, or Ctrl+Space to toggle between playing and pausing the track. **Next** and **Previous** buttons are next to the Play/Pause button. Click on these buttons to play the next and previous songs in your library or playlist. Rhythmbox also has options to toggle repeat mode (**Repeat**, **Control ▸ Repeat** or Ctrl+R) and shuffle mode (**Shuffle**, **Control ▸ Shuffle** or Ctrl+U).

Playing Audio CDs

To play your CD, insert it into your CD drive. It will automatically appear within Rhythmbox in the *Side Pane* beneath your Music Library. You can click the CD (named Audio CD, or the name of the album) and double-click a track in it to play the tracks on the CD.

Importing (Ripping) Audio CDs

Begin by inserting a CD. Rhythmbox will automatically detect it and add it to the side menu. If you have an active Internet connection, Rhythmbox will try to find the album details via the web. Click the CD. Uncheck any tracks you don't want imported. Press the **Extract** button, located at the *upper-left* corner of the right panel. Rhythmbox will begin importing the CD. As it finishes each track, it will appear in your Music Library.

Listening to streaming audio

Rhythmbox is pre-configured to enable you to stream audio from various sources. These include Internet broadcast stations (**Radio** from the Side Pane), **Last.fm** and **Libre.fm**. To listen to an Internet radio station, click on the Radio icon in the *Side Pane* for a list of pre-configured stations. You can filter by genre in the *middle pane*. To add a new radio station, select **Add** and enter the radio station URL.

Streaming audio stations are "radio stations" that broadcast over the Internet. Some of these are real radio stations that also stream over the Internet, and others broadcast only over the Internet.

You can browse a selected list of radio stations at http://en.wikipedia.org/wiki/List_of_Internet_stations or you can use your browser to search for "Internet radio stations."

Connect digital audio players

Rhythmbox can connect with many popular digital media players. Connected players will appear in the *Devices list*. Features will vary depending on the player (and often the player's popularity), but common tasks like transferring songs and playlists should be supported.

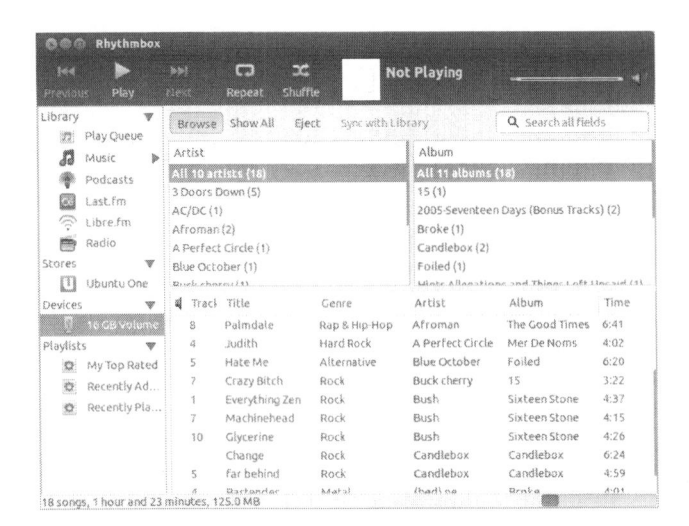

Figure 3.29: Rhythmbox connected to an Android device

Listen to shared music

If you are on the same network as other Rhythmbox users (or most other music player software), you can share your music and listen to their shared music. To do this, click **Music ▸ Connect to DAAP Share...** Then enter the IP address and the port number. Click **OK**. Clicking a shared library will enable you to browse and play songs from other computers.

DAAP stands for "Digital Audio Access Protocol," and is a method designed by Apple to let software share media across a network.

Manage podcasts

Rhythmbox can manage all of your favorite podcasts. Select *Podcasts* from the Side Pane to view all added podcasts. The toolbar will display additional options to *Browse*, *Show All*, *Add* and *Update*. Choose **Add** on the toolbar and enter the URL of the podcasts to save it to Rhythmbox. Podcasts will be automatically downloaded at regular intervals or you can manually update feeds. Select an episode and click **Play**. You can also delete episodes.

Party mode

Rhythmbox comes with the option of a "party mode." To enter party mode press F11 on your keyboard or use the global menu bar (**View ▸ Party Mode**); to exit from party mode press F11 again. Rhythmbox also has a browser bar that is enabled by default (this area is the top-right half of the program window). It gives you the option to search your music by artist or album.

Rhythmbox preferences

The default configuration of Rhythmbox may not be exactly what you want. Choose **Edit ▸ Preferences** to alter the application settings. The Preferences tool is broken into four main areas: general, playback, music, and Podcasts.

General includes how you want Rhythmbox to display artist and track information. You can adjust the columns visible in your library and how the toolbar icons are displayed.

Playback options allow you to enable crossfading and the duration of the fade between tracks.

Music includes where you would like to place your music files and the library structure for new tracks added to Rhythmbox. You can also set your preferred audio format.

Podcasts designates where podcasts are stored on your computer along with the ability to change how often podcast information is updated.

Plugins

Rhythmbox supports a wide array of plugins, which add functionality to Rhythmbox. Many of the plugins provide basic audio playback, and you may check a few more boxes, for example, to access the Magnatune Store. To view or change the activated plugins, use the global menu bar (**Edit ▸ Plugins**).

Managing your music

Rhythmbox supports creating playlists. *Playlists* either are static lists of songs to be played in order, or can be smart playlists based on filter criteria. Playlists contain references to songs in your library. They do not contain the actual songs, but only reference them. So, if you remove a song from a playlist (**right-click on the song ▸ Remove from Playlist**), the song will remain in your library and on your hard drive.

To create a playlist, choose **Music ▸ Playlist ▸ New Playlist**, press Ctrl+N, or right-click in the lower blank area of the side bar and select **New Playlist**. It appears in the sidebar as "New Playlist." Right-click and select **Rename** to give the new playlist a name of your choosing. Drag songs from your library to the new playlist in the side pane or right-click on songs and select **Add to Playlist** and pick the playlist.

Smart Playlists are created in a similar way. Choose **Music ▸ Playlist ▸ New Automatic Playlist** or right-click in the lower blank area of the side bar and select **New Automatic Playlist**. Define the filter criteria. You can add multiple filter rules and select a name. Save. You can update any playlist (including the predefined ones) by right-clicking on the name and choosing Edit.

Rhythmbox supports song ratings. **Right-click a song in your library ▸ Properties ▸ Details** and click on the number of stars. To remove a rating, select zero stars. Other song information such as Title, Artist and Album can be changed. **Right-click a song in your library ▸ Properties ▸ Basic**.

To remove a song, **right-click ▸ Remove**. To delete a song from your hard drive entirely, **right-click ▸ Move to the Rubbish Bin**. If you ever want to move a song, highlight the song (or group of songs) from your library and drag it to a folder or to your desktop. This will make a copy of the audio file in the new location.

Music stores

Rhythmbox has an integrated store that gives you access to a huge catalog of music with a variety of licensing options. The *Ubuntu One Music Store* (see figure below) sells music from global major and minor music labels. The store offers *DRM-free* (no copy protection) songs encoded in high-quality MP3 format. You can browse the catalog, play previews, and buy songs with the Ubuntu One Music Store. As the name suggests, the Ubuntu One Music Store integrates with the Ubuntu One service. All purchases are transferred to your personal cloud storage and are automatically copied to all of your computers. For that reason, an Ubuntu One account is required (it is free of charge and quick to register). The catalog of music available for purchase will vary depending on where you live in the world. More information about the Ubuntu One Music Store can be found at https://one.ubuntu.com/music/.

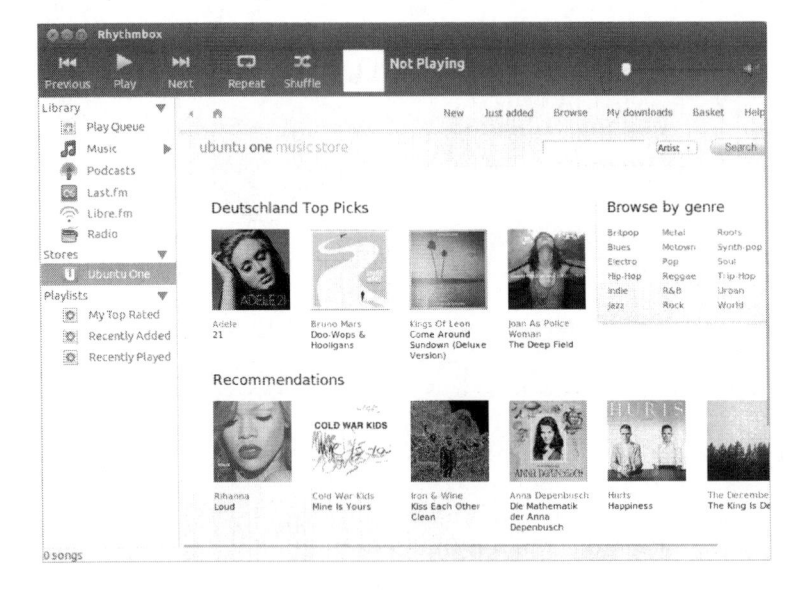

Figure 3.30: Ubuntu One Music Store

Audio codecs

Different audio files (MP3, WAV, AAC, OGG, etc.) require unique tools to decode them and play the contents. These tools are called *codecs*. Rhythmbox attempts to detect any missing codecs on your system so you can play all of your audio files. If a codec is missing, it automatically tries to find the codec online and guides you through its installation.

Rhythmbox support

Rhythmbox is used by many users throughout the world. There are a variety of support resources available in many languages.

- **Help ▸ Contents** or F1 for the main help.
- **Help ▸ Get Help Online** to ask questions and report bugs.
- The Rhythmbox website at http://www.rhythmbox.org/.
- The Multimedia & Video category of Ubuntu Forums at http://ubuntuforums.org/forumdisplay.php?f=334.

Burning CDs and DVDs

To create a CD or DVD, open the Dash and search for `Brasero Disc Burner`. Once you find Brasero, double-click it. This opens Brasero application. The burning options that now appear are explained below.

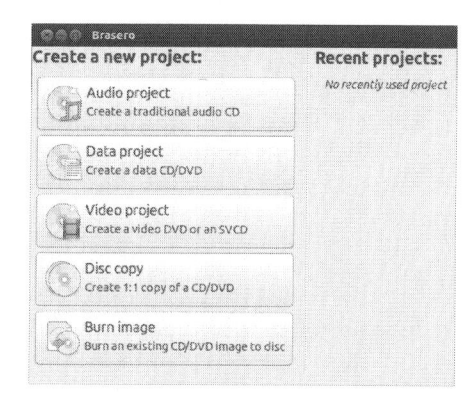

Figure 3.31: Brasero burns music, video, data DVDs and CDs.

Getting Started

Before you can use Brasero, you need to **Create a new project**. There are three types of projects available: Audio Project, Data Project, and Video Project. Make your selection based on your requirements.

The following options apply for all projects except **Disc copy** and **Burn Image**.

At this current time, Brasero does not support Blu-Ray.

Adding files to a project

To add files to the list, click the **Green +** button, which opens the "Select Files" window. Then navigate your way to the file you want to add, click the desired file, and then click the **Add** button. Repeat this process for each file until all desired files have been added.

Removing files

If you want to remove a file from the project, click the file in the list and click on the **Red -** button. To remove all the files in the list click on the **Broom** shaped button.

Icons of a broom are often used in Ubuntu to represent clearing a text field or returning something to its default state.

Saving a project

To save an unfinished project, choose **Project ▸ Save**. The "Save Current Project" window will be opened. Choose where you would like to save the project. In the **Name:** text field, enter a name for the project. Click the **Save** button, and your unfinished project is saved. When saving a project, you are only saving the parameters of the project; you've burned nothing to the disc at this time.

Burning the disc

When you click the **Burn...** button, you will see the "Properties of ..." window.

You can specify the burning speed in the **Burning speed** drop-down. It is best to choose the highest speed.

To burn your project directly to the disc, select the **Burn the image directly without saving it to disc** option. With this option selected, no image file is created, and no files are saved to the hard disk. All data is saved to the blank CD or DVD.

The **Simulate before burning** option is useful if you encounter problems burning discs. Selecting this option allows you to simulate the disc burning process without actually writing data to a disc—a wasteful process if your computer isn't writing data correctly. If the simulation is successful, Brasero will burn the disc after a ten second pause. During those ten seconds, you have the option to cancel the burning process.

> Temporary files are saved in the /tmp folder by default. Should you wish to save these files in another location, you will need to change the setting in the **Temporary files** drop-down menu. Under normal conditions, you should not need to change this setting.

Blanking a disk

If you are using a disc that has RW written on it and you have used it before, then you can erase it so that it can be reused. Erasing a disc simply deletes all of the data currently on the disc. To erase a disc, open the **Tools** menu, then select **Blank**. The "Disc Blanking" window will be open. In the **Select a disc** drop-down choose the disc that you would like to erase.

You can enable the **Fast blank** option if you would like to shorten the amount of time to perform the blanking process. However, selecting this option will not fully remove the files; if you have any sensitive data on your disc, it would be best not to enable the **Fast blank** option.

Once the disc is erased (blank), you will see *The disc was successfully blanked.* Click the **Close** button to finish.

> RW stands for *Re-Writable* which means the disc can be used more than once.

Audio project

If you record your own music, then you may want to transfer this music onto an audio CD so your friends and family can listen. You can start an audio project by clicking **Project ▸ New Project ▸ New Audio Project**.

When burning a music CD, it is important to remember that commercial music CDs usually have two-second gap between song. To ensure your music has this same gap between songs, click the file and then click the **pause** button.

You can slice files into parts by clicking the **Knife** button. This opens a "Split Track" window. The **Method** drop-down gives you four options; each option lets you split the track in a different way. Once you have split the track, click **OK**.

In the drop-down list at the bottom of the main "Brasero" window, make sure that you have selected the disc where you want to burn the files. Then click the **Burn** button.

Data project

If you want to make a back up of your documents or photos, it would be best to make a data project. You can start a data project by clicking **Project ▸ New Project ▸ New Data Project.**

If you want to add a folder you can click the **Folder** picture, then enter the name of the folder.

In the drop-down list at the bottom of the main "Brasero" window, be sure to select the disc where you want to burn the files. Then click the **Burn** button.

Video project

If you want to make a DVD of your family videos, it would be best to make a video project.

You can start a video project by clicking **Project ▸ New Project ▸ New Video Project.**

In the drop-down list at the bottom of the main "Brasero" window, be sure to select the disc where you want to burn the files. Then click the **Burn** button.

Disc copy

You can copy a disc clicking **Project ▸ New Project ▸ Disc copy.** This opens the "Copy CD/DVD" window.

If you have two CD/DVD drives, you can copy a disc from one to the other, assuming the source disc is in one drive and the destination disc (with blank media) is in the other drive. If you have only one drive you will need to make an image and then burn it to a disc. In the **Select disc to copy** drop-down choose the disc to copy. In the **Select a disc to write to** drop-down either choose image file or the disc that you want to copy to.

> An image is a single-file representation of the contents of the disk. The file usually has an .iso or .img extension. An image file is similar a set of zipped files.

Image file

You can change where the image file is saved by clicking **Properties.** This shows the "Location for Image File". You can edit the name of the file in the **Name:** text field.

The default location to save the image file is your home folder, but you can change the location by clicking the + button next to **Browse for other folders.** Once you have chosen where you want to save the photo or image, click **Close.**

Returning to the "Copy CD/DVD" window, click **Create Image.** Brasero will open the "Creating Image" and will display the job progress. When the process is complete, click **Close.**

Burn image

To burn an image, open the **Project ▸ New Project ▸ Burn Image.** Brasero will open the "Image Burning Setup" window. Click on the **Click here to select a disc image** drop-down and the "Select Disc Image" window will appear. Navigate your way to the image you wish to burn, click on it, and then click **Open.**

In the **Select a disc to write to** drop-down menu, click on the disc to which you'd like to write, then click **Create Image**.

Working with documents, spreadsheets, and presentations

LibreOffice Suite is the default office suite when working with documents, spreadsheets, and slide presentations.

Working with documents

If you need to work with documents, you can use the LibreOffice Word Processor. To start the word processor, open the Dash and search for `LibreOffice Writer`. Then select **LibreOffice Writer**.

The LibreOffice Word Processor is also known as the LibreOffice Writer. LibreOffice Spreadsheet is also known as Calc, and LibreOffice Presentation is known as Impress.

Working with spreadsheets

If you need to work with spreadsheets, you can use LibreOffice Spreadsheet. To start the spreadsheet application, open the Dash and search for `LibreOffice Calc`. Then select **LibreOffice Calc**.

Working with presentations

If you need to work with slides for a presentation, you can use LibreOffice Impress. To start the presentation application, open the Dash and search for `LibreOffice Impress`. Then select **LibreOffice Impress**.

Getting more help

Each of these applications comes with a comprehensive set of help screens. If you are looking for more assistance with these applications, press the F1 key after starting the application.

Ubuntu One

What is Ubuntu One?

Ubuntu One is a service for storing your files online—in your Ubuntu One *Personal Cloud*. Your Ubuntu One Personal Cloud is your personal online storage space; it can be accessed in any web browser or using an Ubuntu One application, such as those for Ubuntu, Windows, iPhone, or Android. Because Ubuntu One stores your files online, it's the perfect way to backup your files to prevent data loss. You can also use Ubuntu One to share files with other people—this makes Ubuntu One a great tool for friends, families, and collaborative teams. Ubuntu One also provides services for backing up your contacts and streaming music to mobile devices. The Ubuntu One service is provided by Canonical.

How safe is Ubuntu One?

Before using Ubuntu One, you should bear the following points in mind:

- Uploading, downloading and synchronizing your information with Ubuntu One is done over an encrypted connection, which prevents anybody eavesdropping on your information as it is being transferred.

- Files are not stored by Canonical in encrypted form. It is important to keep this in mind when deciding what to upload to Ubuntu One. You can use other means to encrypt you data, such as an encrypted zip file.
- Information uploaded to Ubuntu One can potentially be accessed by Canonical. As with similar online services and websites, you are implicitly trusting them to respect your privacy, so if you feel you cannot trust them with certain information, don't upload it to Ubuntu One.
- If you violate the Ubuntu One terms and conditions and store illegal material, Canonical may be required to hand the information over to law enforcement agencies without your consent.
- Your online information can be accessed by anybody who knows (or can guess) your account name and password. For this reason, you should choose a good password and keep it secure.

Getting started with Ubuntu One

To use Ubuntu One, you will need to create a free Ubuntu One account using an email address. This free account gives you access to 5 GB of online storage and the contact syncing service; access to more data storage or the music streaming service requires a paid subscription.

There are two ways to create an Ubuntu One account. You can either sign up using the Ubuntu One Control Panel (pre-installed in Ubuntu), or you can sign up on the Ubuntu One website https://one.ubuntu.com by clicking the **Sign Up** link.

5 GB is enough to store about 1,500 music files or 5,000 photographs (depending on size).

Figure 3.32: This Launcher icon opens the Ubuntu One Control Panel.

Creating an Ubuntu One account using the Ubuntu One Control Panel

In the Launcher, click the **Ubuntu One** icon, as shown in figure 3.32. This should open the dialog shown in figure 3.33.

Figure 3.33: The Ubuntu One Control Panel Welcome Page.

Click the **I don't have an account yet – sign me up** button.

Fill in the details requested as shown in figure 3.34. Make sure you use a valid email address that only you have access to.

You should review the **Terms of Service** and **Privacy Policy** before signing up. When you're satisfied, click **Set Up Account**.

Within a few minutes, you will receive an email containing the verification code. Enter the verification code into the box as shown in figure 3.35 and click **Next**.

If you do not have an email address, you can get one for free at gmail.com.

The captcha acts as a check that it really is a person filling in the form and not a computer (because a computer won't be able to read the captcha text).

Figure 3.34: Fill in all fields with your information to sign up for an Ubuntu One account.

Figure 3.35: Enter the verification code into the field.

If all goes well, you will see a window saying, "You are now logged into Ubuntu One." Click the **Finish** button to dismiss this window. You will also get another email welcoming you to Ubuntu One. Now that you are logged in to Ubuntu One, you can configure your Ubuntu machine for Ubuntu One file syncing.

Configure your Ubuntu machine for file syncing

The Ubuntu One desktop application *syncs* your Ubuntu One Personal Cloud with files on your local file system. After logging into the Ubuntu One desktop application the following dialog (figure 3.36) should appear, allowing you to select which files to sync with your Ubuntu One Personal Cloud.

If you have already used your Ubuntu One account, you may have more folders in this view (figure 3.36). You can choose which Ubuntu One cloud folders you would like synced with your local file system. If this is the first time you are using Ubuntu One, just click the **Next** button.

Sync is short for Synchronize; implying that the contents of your Ubuntu One local file system and your Ubuntu One Personal Cloud will always be identical.

> You can also change your Ubuntu One sync connection settings at this time by clicking on the **Check Settings** button; you can change things like the maximum upload and download rate, or if notifications should be allowed.

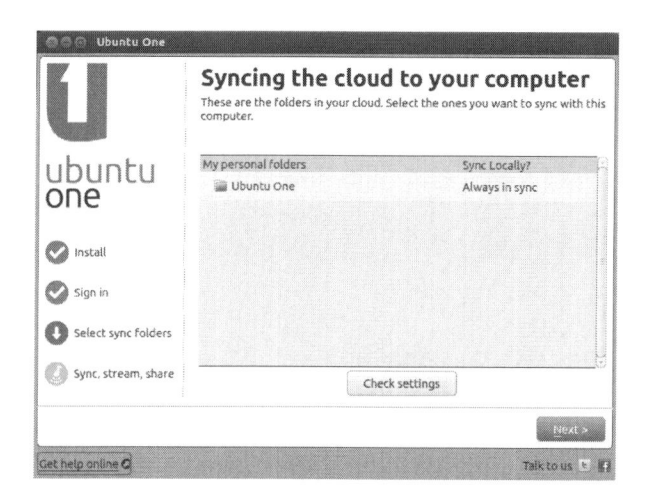

Figure 3.36: This setup dialog lets you select which existing Ubuntu One folders you would like synced with your machine.

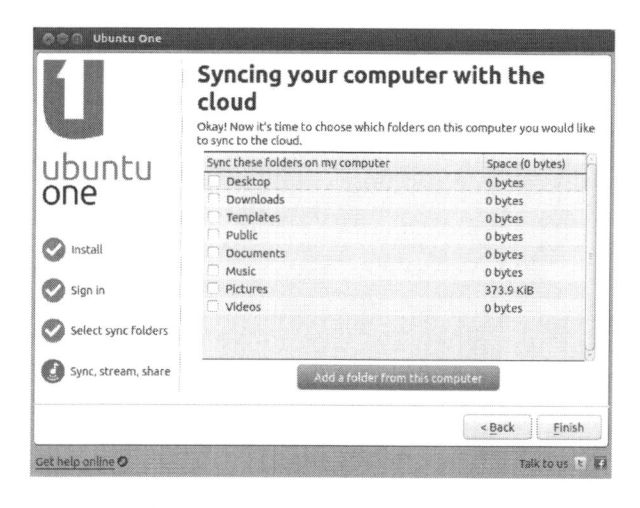

Figure 3.37: This setup dialog lets you select which folders of your local file system you would like synced with your Ubuntu One cloud storage.

In the next dialog (figure 3.37), you can choose which of your local file system folders you would like synced with your Ubuntu One cloud storage. The folder *Ubuntu One* is implicitly synced, but you can select additional folders you may like synced—your pictures, for instance. Once you're finished selecting folders, click the **Finish** button to complete the setup process. You are now ready to begin using Ubuntu One!

Using Ubuntu One with the Nautilus file manager

Ubuntu One integrates with the Nautilus file browser, the program you use to view your file system. You can add, sync, and share files directly from Nautilus.

Adding and Modifying Files

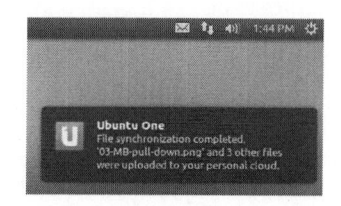

Figure 3.38: These symbols indicate the sync status of a file or folder. The Checkmark indicates that the file or folder has been synced, and the circular arrows indicate that the file or folder is in the process of syncing.

Figure 3.39: When you add files to an Ubuntu One synced folder, they automatically sync to your personal cloud.

You can add files to your Ubuntu One folder (or any other folder that you have selected for sync) just as you normally would, and Ubuntu One will automatically sync them to your personal cloud. For example, if you add your vacation photos, you should see a notification message on the screen similar to figure 3.39.

After moving the files into the Ubuntu One synced folder, you should receive a notification informing you that syncing has begun. You can also see that each file shows the circular arrow icon, indicating that it is currently syncing with your personal cloud. When syncing completes, the circular arrows will be replaced with check marks.

Whenever you add or modify files that are in folders synced with Ubuntu One, they will automatically sync to your personal cloud. After syncing is complete, you can view the files on the Ubuntu One Web UI, and they will also be synced to any other computers or mobile devices that you are using Ubuntu One on.

Adding Folders to Sync

You can add other folders to be synced with your Ubuntu One Personal Cloud, not just your *Ubuntu One* folder. You can add folders to be synced through Nautilus by right-clicking the folder you would like to sync. In the right-click menu, choose **Ubuntu One ▸ Synchronize This Folder**, as shown in figure 3.40. You can also stop syncing a folder through the same right-click menu.

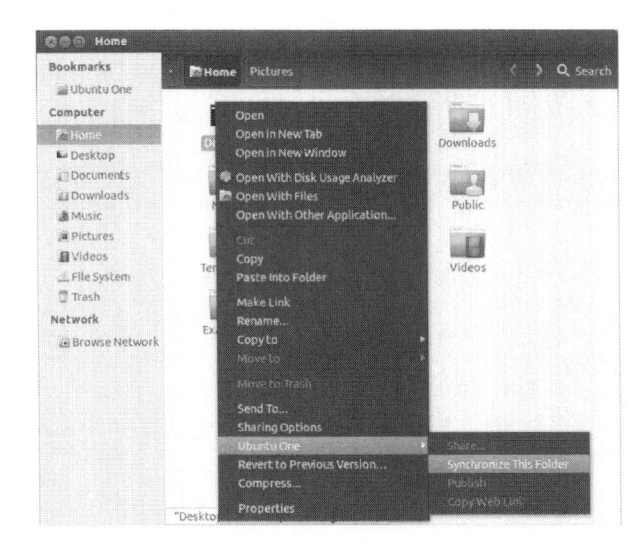

Figure 3.40: Use a folder's right-click menu to sync or un-sync the folder from your Ubuntu One Personal Cloud.

To view which files on your system are are currently syncing with Ubuntu One, open the Ubuntu One Control Panel by clicking the **Ubuntu One** Launcher icon, as shown in figure 3.32; a dialog similar to that in figure 3.41 should appear.

In the Ubuntu One Control Panel you can see which of your folders are synced with your Ubuntu One Personal Cloud. You can also add files from here, by clicking the **Add a folder from this computer** button.

Using Ubuntu One with the Ubuntu One Web UI

You can access your files from any computer using the Ubuntu One Web UI at https://one.ubuntu.com. When you first reach the web page, you will need to log in by clicking **Log in or Sign up** in the upper right-hand corner

A *Web UI* (User Interface) is a web site that you can go to and do the same things that you do on your computer. Emails, for instance, are commonly accessed through a Web UI.

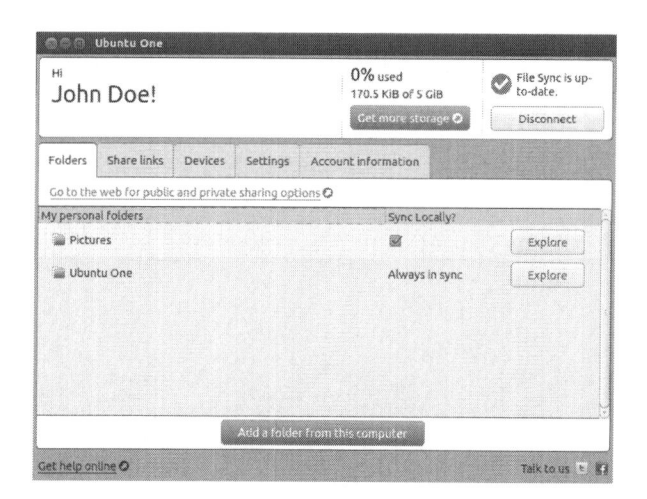

Figure 3.41: The Ubuntu One Control Panel shows you which folders in your file system are synced with your Ubuntu One Personal Cloud.

of the page. On the following page, fill in your email address and Ubuntu One password, then click the **Continue** button.

Once logged in, you should be taken to your *Dashboard*. The Dashboard shows you a summary of your data usage, and keeps you informed of new features in Ubuntu One.

To view your files, click the **Files** link in the navigation bar in the upper portion of the page.

Downloading and Uploading Files

To access your files from the Ubuntu One Web UI, you can simply download them from your personal cloud. To download a file, click **More** shown to the right of the file, as shown in the browser, then click on **Download file**, as shown in figure 3.42. Clicking **Download file** will initiate a file download through your browser.

If you make changes to the file or want to add a new file to your personal cloud, simply click the **Upload file** button in the upper portion of the page. This will upload the file into the current folder and overwrite any old versions of the file. Once you have uploaded the file, it will be available in your personal cloud, and will sync to your Ubuntu machine's local file system.

Making Files Public

You can make a file public on the web by clicking **More** and choosing the **Publish file** button—this is also shown in figure 3.42. After clicking the **Publish file** button, the Web UI will generate a *Public URL*; you can share this URL with anyone. By directing a browser to the Public URL of the file, the browser will begin to download the file or display it, depending on what type of file it is.

You can make the file private again at any time by clicking the **Stop publishing** button located to the left of the Public URL. After you click the **Stop publishing** button the Public URL field will go away, and the URL will stop working. If someone tries to use a Public URL for a file that has been made private, they will receive an error message and the file will not be downloaded or displayed.

The Ubuntu One Contol Panel lists all of your public files in one place under the **Share links** tab. This is a convenient way to keep tabs on which

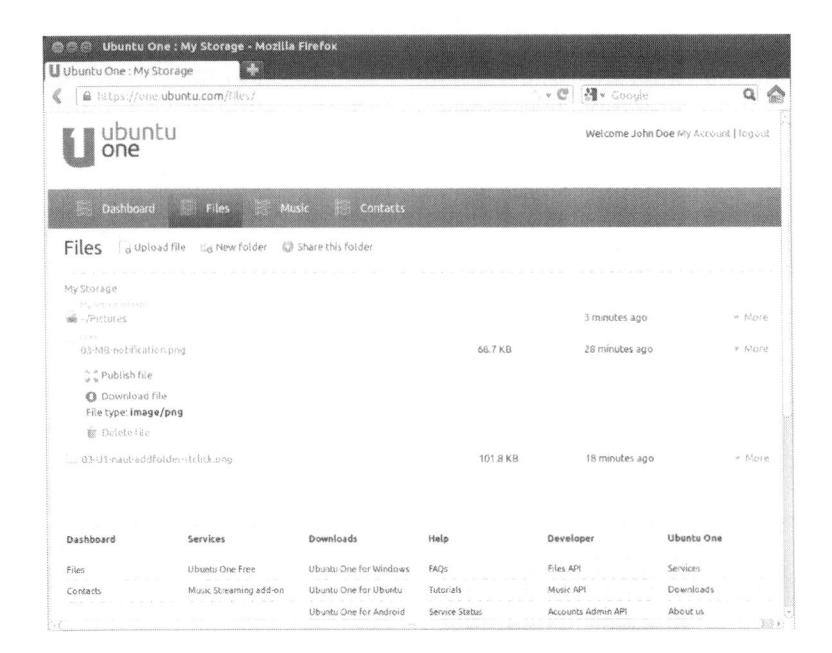

Figure 3.42: A file's **More** button in the Web UI gives you many options.

files you are publishing, and allows you to easily copy their links by clicking the **Copy link** button located next to each public file.

Sharing Files

Ubuntu One lets you share files with other Ubuntu One users, letting you collaborate on files with ease. When one user makes a change to a shared file the changes automatically sync to the other users' personal clouds and their local file system, so all users automatically have the most recent version of the file.

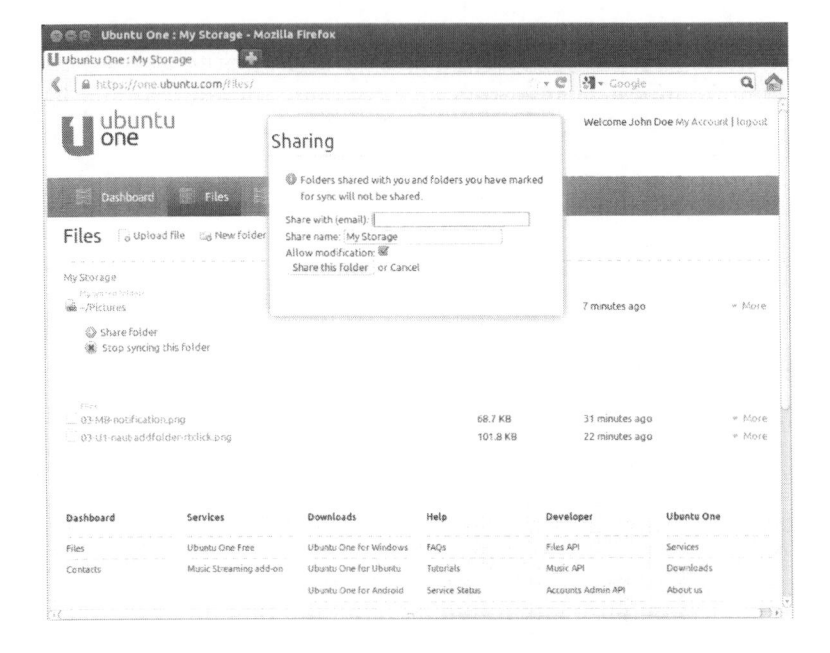

Figure 3.43: Sharing folders with other users makes collaborating on files simple.

To share files in Ubuntu One, you must share an entire folder. Before you begin to share files, you should make sure only the files you want to share

are in this folder. Then to share this folder, navigate to it in the Ubuntu One Web UI, and click the **More** button to the right of the folder name. In the **More** menu, click on **Share folder**. A dialog box similar to that shown in figure 3.43 should appear. Complete the fields in the dialog box, and click the **Share this folder** button when you are finished.

Once you share the folder, the user you are trying to share the folder with should receive an email informing them that you would like to share the file. They will then have to accept the share request. If the email address you provide does not yet have an Ubuntu One account, they must first sign up for an Ubuntu One account before they can access the shared folder.

To stop sharing a folder, navigate to it, click the **More** button, and click **Stop sharing**.

If another user shares a folder with you, you will receive an email informing you of the share, and a link to click on to accept the share request. Folders that are shared with you by other users will appear in the *Shared With Me* folder inside your Ubuntu One folder (`~/Ubuntu One/Shared With Me/`).

To stop syncing files that are shared with you, navigate to the folder in the Ubuntu One Web UI, click the **More** button, then click the **Delete this share** button.

Exceeding your Ubuntu One Storage Limit

If you exceed the storage limit of your Ubuntu One account—5 GB is the free limit—Ubuntu One will stop syncing your files to your Ubuntu One Personal Cloud.

Remedying an Exceeded Storage Limit

You can do several things to remedy an exceeded storage limit. Among them are:

- Delete any files you no longer need.
- Move any files you no longer need synced to another location that is not synced with Ubuntu One.
- Purchase additional storage space—you can purchase additional storage in 20 GB blocks.

Purchasing Additional Storage Space

You can purchase additional storage space by clicking the **Get more storage** button in the Ubuntu One Control Panel, or at https://one.ubuntu.com/services/. Additional storage is available in 20 GB blocks. See https://one.ubuntu.com/services/ for the price of additional storage blocks.

Getting Ubuntu One Mobile Apps

86   GETTING STARTED WITH UBUNTU 12.10

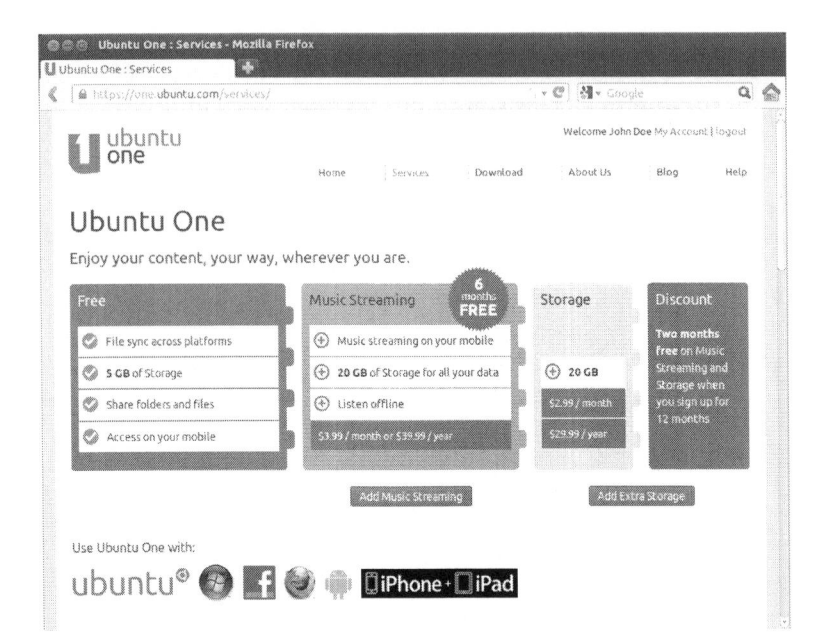

Figure 3.44: You can purchase additional storage space on the Ubuntu One website. Note that the prices shown here were correct at the date this manual was published.

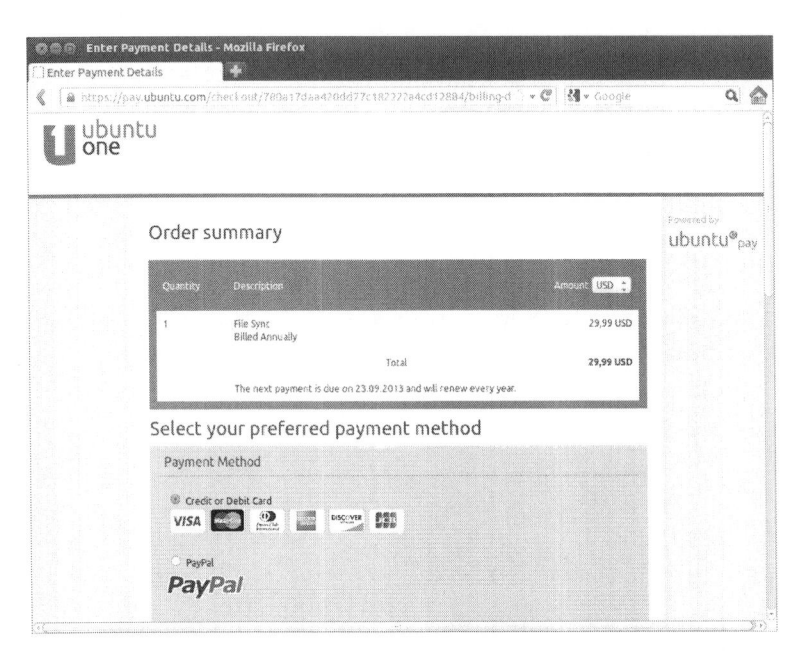

Figure 3.45: Ubuntu One accepts credit cards, and PayPal for purchasing additional storage.

Ubuntu One has mobile applications for Android and iPhone mobile devices. These applications allow you to access your personal cloud files on-the-go. You can get more information about the Android and iPhone applications at https://one.ubuntu.com/downloads/android/ and https://one.ubuntu.com/downloads/iphone/, respectively.

Figure 3.46: This is the icon for the Ubuntu One Android and iPhone apps.

Getting Ubuntu One for Windows

Ubuntu One also has a Windows application, which can sync your Ubuntu One Personal Cloud files to the file system of a Windows operating system. More information can be found at https://one.ubuntu.com/downloads/windows/.

Additional Services of Ubuntu One

In addition to file syncing, Ubuntu One offers Contact Syncing and Music Streaming services. These services are not discussed in this book, but additional information can be found at https://one.ubuntu.com/help/tutorial/contact-sync-for-ubuntu-1004-lts/ and https://one.ubuntu.com/services/music/ respectively. The Music Streaming service requires a paid subscription, but it has a 30 day free trial period during which you can cancel with nothing to pay. See https://one.ubuntu.com/services/ for the price of the Music Streaming service.

4 Hardware

Using your devices

Ubuntu supports a wide range of hardware, and support for new hardware improves with every release.

Hardware identification

There are various ways to identify your hardware in Ubuntu. The easiest would be to install an application from the **Ubuntu Software Center**, called Sysinfo.

Firstly, open the "Ubuntu Software Center", then use the search box in the top right corner to search for `sysinfo`. Select the Application, click **Install**. Enter your password when prompted, to install the application.

To run the application, search for Sysinfo at the Dash search bar. Click on the program once you find it. The Sysinfo program will open a window that displays information about the hardware in your system.

Displays

Hardware drivers

A driver is a piece of software which tells your computer how to communicate with a piece of hardware. Every component in a computer requires a driver to function, whether it's the printer, DVD player, hard disk, or graphics card.

The majority of graphics cards are manufactured by three well-known companies: Intel, AMD/ATI, and NVIDIA Corp. You can find your video card manufacturer by referring to your computer's manual, by looking for the specifications of your computer's model on the Internet, or by using the command `lspci` in a terminal. The Ubuntu Software Center houses a number of applications that can tell you detailed system information. SysInfo is one such program that you can use to find relevant information about your System devices. Ubuntu comes with support for graphics devices manufactured by the above companies, and many others, out of the box. That means you don't have to find and install any drivers yourself, Ubuntu takes care of it all.

Keeping in line with Ubuntu's philosophy, the drivers that are used by default for powering graphics devices are open source. This means that the drivers can be modified by the Ubuntu developers and problems with them can be fixed. However, in some cases a proprietary driver (restricted driver) provided by the company may provide better performance or features that are not present in the open source driver. In other cases, your particular device may not be supported by any open source drivers yet. In those scenarios, you may want to install the restricted driver provided by the manufacturer.

For both philosophical and practical reasons, Ubuntu does not install restricted drivers by default but allows the user to make an informed choice. Remember that restricted drivers, unlike the open source drivers for your device, are not maintained by Ubuntu. Problems caused by those drivers

> Your graphics card is the component in your computer which outputs to the display. Whether you are watching videos on YouTube, viewing DVDs, or simply enjoying the smooth transition effects when you maximize/minimize your windows, your graphics device is doing the hard work behind the scenes.

will be resolved only when the manufacturer wishes to address them. To see if restricted drivers are available for your system, press the Super/Windows key on your keyboard to show the Dash or click the Ubuntu icon on the Unity Launcher, and search for `Additional Drivers`. If a driver is provided by the company for your particular device, it will be listed there. You can simply click **Activate** to enable the driver. This process requires an active Internet connection and it will ask for your password. Once installation is complete you may have to reboot your computer to finish activating the driver.

The Ubuntu developers prefer open source drivers because they allow any problem to be identified and fixed by anyone with knowledge within the community. Ubuntu development is extremely fast and it is likely that your device will be supported by open source drivers. You can use the Ubuntu Live DVD to check your device's compatibility with Ubuntu before installing, or go online to the Ubuntu forums or to http://www.askubuntu.com to ask about your particular device.

Another useful resource is the official online documentation (http://help.ubuntu.com), which contains detailed information about various graphics drivers and known problems. This same documentation can be found by searching for `Yelp` in the Dash search bar or by pressing F1 on your keyboard.

Setting up your screen resolution

One of the most common display related tasks is setting the correct screen resolution for your desktop monitor or laptop.

Ubuntu correctly identifies your native screen resolution by itself and sets it for you. However, due to a wide variety of devices available, sometimes it can't properly identify your resolution.

To set or check your screen resolution, go to **System Settings ▸ Displays**. The "Displays" window detects automatically the type of display and shows your display's name, size. The screen resolution and refresh rate is set to the recommended value by Ubuntu. If the recommended settings are not to your liking, you can change the same from the **Resolution** drop-down to the resolution of your choice.

Displays are made up of thousands of tiny pixels. Each pixel displays a different color, and when combined they all display the image that you see. The native screen resolution is a measure of the amount of actual pixels on your display.

Adding an extra display

Sometimes, you may want to add more than one display device to your desktop, or may want to add an external monitor to your laptop. Doing this is quite simple. Whether it's an extra monitor, LCD TV, or a projector, Ubuntu can handle it all. Ubuntu supports the addition of multiple displays by default, which is as easy as plug and play. Ubuntu recognizes almost all the latest monitors, TVs and projectors by default. Sometimes it may happen that your additional display is not detected when you connect it to the machine. To resolve this, go to **System Settings ▸ Displays** and click on **Detect Displays**. This will detect the monitors connected to the machine. This menu can also be found from the **Power Off** menu on the top panel. You can also search for Displays at the Dash search bar. Now, there are two modes which you can enable for your displays. One option is to spread your desktop across two or more monitors. This is particularly useful if you are working on multiple projects and need to keep an eye on each of them at the same time. The second option is to mirror the desktop onto each of the displays. This is particularly useful when you are using a laptop to display something on a larger screen or a projector. To enable this option just check the box beside **Mirror displays** and click **Apply** to save the settings. You will get a pop-up notification asking if you want to keep the current setting or revert to the previous setting. Click to keep the current setting.

Starting from Ubuntu 12.04, you can also select whether you want the Unity Launcher in both the displays or only in the primary display.

Connecting and using your printer

Ubuntu supports most new printers. You can add, remove, and change printer properties by navigating to **System Settings ▸ Printing**. You can also search for Printing from the Dash search bar. Opening Printing will display the "Printing-localhost" window.

When you want to add a printer, you will need to make sure that it is switched on, and plugged into your computer with a USB cable or connected to your network.

Adding a local printer

If you have a printer that is connected to your computer with a USB cable then this is termed a *local printer*. You can add a printer by clicking on the **Add Printer** button.

In the left hand pane of the "New Printer" window any printers that you can install will be listed. Select the printer that you would like to install and click **Forward**.

You can now specify the printer name, description and location. Each of these should remind you of that particular printer so that you can choose the right one to use when printing. Finally, click **Apply**.

Adding a network printer

Make sure that your printer is connected to your network either with an Ethernet cable or via wireless and is turned on. You can add a printer by clicking **Add Printer**. The "New Printer" window will open. Click the "+" sign next to *Network Printer*.

If your printer is found automatically it will appear under *Network Printer*. Click the printer name and then click **Forward**. In the text fields you can now specify the printer name, description and location. Each of these should remind you of that particular printer so that you can choose the right one to use when printing. Finally click **Apply**.

You can also add your network printer by entering the IP address of the printer. Select "Find Network Printer," enter the IP address of the printer in the box that reads **Host:** and press the **Find** button. Ubuntu will find the printer and add it. Most printers are detected by Ubuntu automatically. If Ubuntu cannot detect the printer automatically, it will ask you to enter the make and model number of the printer.

> If your printer can automatically do double sided printing, it will probably have a duplexer. Please refer to the instructions that came with the printer if you are unsure. If you do have a duplexer, make sure the **Duplexer Installed** option is checked and then click the **Forward** button.

> The default printer is the one that is automatically selected when you print a file. To set a printer as default, right-click the printer that you want to set as default and then click **Set As Default**.

Changing printer options

Printer options allow you to change the printing quality, paper size and media type. They can be changed by right-clicking a printer and choosing **Properties**. The "Printer Properties" window will show; in the left pane, select *Printer Options*.

You can now specify settings by changing the drop-down entries. Some of the options that you might see are explained.

Media size

This is the size of the paper that you put into your printer tray.

Media source

This is the tray that the paper comes from.

Color Model

This is very useful if you want to print in **Grayscale** to save on ink, or to print in **Color**, or **Inverted Grayscale**.

Media type

Depending on the printer you can change between:

- Plain Paper
- Automatic
- Photo Paper
- Transparency Film
- CD or DVD Media

Print quality

This specifies how much ink is used when printing, **Fast Draft** using the least ink and **High-Resolution Photo** using the most ink.

Sound

Ubuntu usually detects the audio hardware of the system automatically during installation. The audio in Ubuntu is provided by a sound server named PulseAudio. The audio preferences are easily configurable with the help of a very easy to use GUI which comes preinstalled with Ubuntu.

Volume icon and Sound Preferences

A volume icon, sitting on the top right corner of the screen, provides quick access to a number of audio related functions. When you left-click on the volume icon you are greeted with four options: A mute option at the very top, a slider button which you can move horizontally to increase/decrease volume, a shortcut to the default music player, Rhythmbox, and an option for accessing the Sound Settings. Selecting *Sound Settings* opens up another window, which provides access to options for changing input and output hardware preferences for speakers, microphones and headphones. It also provides options for setting the volume level for each application. Sound Settings can also be found from **System Settings**. It is known as *Sound*.

Output The *Output* tab will have a list of all the sound cards available in your system. Usually there is only one listed; however, if you have a graphics card which supports HDMI audio, it will also show up in the list. The *Output* tab is used for configuring the output of audio. You can increase/decrease and mute/unmute output volume and select your preferred output device. If you have more than one output device, it will be listed in the section which reads "Choose a device for sound output." The default output hardware, which is automatically detected by Ubuntu during installation will be selected. This section also allows you to change the balance of sound on the left and right speakers of your desktop/laptop.

A microphone is used for making audio/video calls which are supported by applications like Skype or Empathy. It can also be used for sound recording.

If you change your sound output device, it will remain as default.

Input The second tab is for configuring audio *Input*. You will be able to use this section when you have an in-built microphone in your system or if you've plugged in an external microphone. You can also add a Bluetooth headset to your input devices which can serve as a microphone. You can increase/decrease and mute/unmute input volume from this tab. If there is more than one input device, you will see them listed in the white box which reads *Choose a device for sound input*.

Sound Effects The third tab is *Sound Effects*. You can enable, disable, or change the existing sound theme from this section. You can also change the alert sounds for different events.

Applications The *Applications* tab is for changing the volume for running applications. This comes in handy if you have multiple audio applications running, for example, if you have Rhythmbox, Totem Movie Player and a web-based video playing at the same time. In this situation, you will be able to increase/decrease, mute/unmute volume for each application from this tab.

More functionality

The icon can control various aspects of the system, application volume and music players like Rhythmbox, Banshee, Clementine and Spotify. The volume indicator icon can now be easily referred to as the sound menu, given the diverse functionality of the icon. Media controls available include play/pause, previous track, and next track. You can also switch between different playlists from the *Choose Playlist* option. There is also a seek bar which you can manually drag to skip some portions of any song. If the current playing song has album art, it will show up beside the name of the current track, otherwise you will see only the details of the song. It displays the track name, the artist name and the album name of the current track.

Using a webcam

Webcams often come built into laptops and netbooks. Some desktops, such as Apple iMacs, have webcams built into their displays. If you purchase a webcam because your computer doesn't have its own, it will most likely have a USB connection. To use a USB webcam, plug it into any empty USB port of your desktop.

Almost all new webcams are detected by Ubuntu automatically. You can configure webcams for individual applications such as Skype and Empathy from the application's setup menu. For webcams which do not work right away with Ubuntu, visit https://wiki.ubuntu.com/Webcam for help.

Scanning text and images

Scanning a document or an image is very simple in Ubuntu. Scanning is handled by the application Simple Scan. Most of the time, Ubuntu will simply detect your scanner and you should just be able to use it. To scan a document, follow these steps:

1. Place what you want to scan on the scanner.
2. Click to open the Dash and enter **scan**.

You should note that by default in any Ubuntu installation, the input sound is muted. You will have to manually unmute to enable your microphone to record sound or use it during audio/video calls.

By default, the volume in Ubuntu is set to maximum during installation.

You can add new sound themes by installing them from Software Center (*e.g.*, Ubuntu Studio's GNOME audio theme.) You will get the installed sound themes from the drop-down menu. You can also enable window and button sounds.

The Ubuntu Design Team have made a few changes to the volume icon post Ubuntu 11.10.

You can start and control the default music player, Rhythmbox, by simply left clicking on the sound menu and selecting Rhythmbox from the list. Clicking the **play** button also starts the player.

There are several applications which are useful if you have a webcam. Cheese can capture pictures with your webcam and VLC media player can capture video from your webcam. You can install these from the Ubuntu Software Center.

3. Click on Simple Scan.
4. Click to choose between **Text** or **Photo** from **Document ▸ Scan ▸ Text**.
5. Click **Scan**.
6. Click the **Paper Icon** to add another page.
7. Click **Save** to save.

You can save the scanned documents and pictures in JPEG. You can also save in PDF format to enable opening in Acrobat Reader. To do that, add the extension .pdf at the end of the filename.

Troubleshooting your scanner

If your scanner is not detected, Ubuntu may give you a "No devices available" message when trying to scan. There may be a reason why Ubuntu cannot find your scanner.

- Simply unplug the scanner and plug it back in. If it is a newer USB scanner, it is likely that it will just work.
- The driver for your scanner is not being automatically loaded. Restart your system. It might help!
- Your scanner is not supported in Ubuntu. The most common type of scanner not supported is old parallel port or Lexmark All-in-One printer/scanner/faxes.
- SANE project listing of supported scanners. The SANE (Scanner Access Now Easy) project provides most of the back-ends to the scanning software on Ubuntu.
- Check https://wiki.ubuntu.com/HardwareSupportComponentsScanners to find out which scanners work with Ubuntu.

Other devices

USB

USB ports are available as standard on almost all computers available now. They are used to connect a multitude of devices to your computer. These could include portable hard drives, flash drives, removable CD/DVD/Blu-ray drives, printers, scanners and mobile phones. When connected, flash drives and portable hard drives are automatically detected—the file manager will open and display the contents of the drive. You can then use the drives for copying data to and from the computer. All new cameras, camcorders and mobile phone SD cards are automatically detected by Ubuntu. These SD cards have different types of data, so a window will appear with a drop-down menu to choose between video, audio import and the file manager —you can choose your desired action from this menu.

Firewire

Firewire is a connection on some computers that allows you to transfer data from devices. This port is generally used by camcorders and digital cameras.

If you want to import video from your camcorder you can do so by connecting your camcorder to the Firewire port. You will need to install a program called Kino which is available in the Ubuntu Software Center.

Firewire is officially known as IEEE 1394. It is also known as the Sony i.LINK and Texas Instruments Lynx.

To find out more about Kino, visit http://www.kinodv.org/.

Bluetooth

Bluetooth is a wireless technology that is widely used by different types of devices to connect to each other. It is common to see a mouse or a keyboard that supports Bluetooth. You can also find GPS devices, mobile phones, headsets, music players and many other devices that can connect to your desktops or laptop and let you transfer data, listen to music, or play games as an example.

If your computer has Bluetooth support then you should see a Bluetooth icon in the top panel, usually near the volume icon. Click on the Bluetooth icon to open a popup menu with several choices, such as an option to **Turn off Bluetooth**.

The Bluetooth preferences can also be accessed from **System Settings ▸ Bluetooth**. If you want to connect a new device—for example, to have a mobile phone send pictures or videos to your computer—select **Setup new device…**.

Ubuntu will open a window for new device setup. When you click **Forward**, Ubuntu will show you how many Bluetooth devices are present near your computer. The list of available devices might take a minute or so to appear on the screen as your system scans for these devices. Each device will be displayed as soon as it is found by Ubuntu. Once a device you'd like to connect with appears in the list, click on it. Then, choose a PIN number by selecting **PIN options**.

Three predefined PIN numbers are available, but you can also create a custom PIN. You will need to enter this PIN on the device you will be pairing with Ubuntu.

Once the device has been paired, Ubuntu will open the "Setup completed" window. In Ubuntu, your computer is hidden by default for security reasons. This means that your Ubuntu system can search other Bluetooth devices, but others cannot find your Ubuntu system when they perform a search on their own computer. If you would like to let another device find your computer, you will have to explicitly allow your computer to be found. To allow your computer to be found, select "Make computer discoverable" in Bluetooth preferences. You can also click on the Bluetooth icon and select **Visible** to make your computer discoverable.

You can also add a fancy name for your Bluetooth-enabled Ubuntu system by changing the text under **Friendly Name**.

Another feature present in the Bluetooth icon menu is "Send files to device." Use this option to send a file to a mobile phone without pairing with the computer.

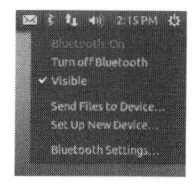

Figure 4.1: The Bluetooth applet menu.

When you *pair* two Bluetooth devices, you are letting each device trust the other one. After you pair two devices, they will automatically connect to each other in the future without requiring a PIN.

Android devices need to be paired at all times, even while transferring files.

5 Software Management

Software management in Ubuntu

As discussed in Chapter 3: Working with Ubuntu, Ubuntu offers a wide range of applications for your daily work. Ubuntu comes with a basic set of applications for common tasks, like surfing the Internet, checking email, listening to music, and organizing photos and videos. Sometimes you may need an extra level of specialization. For example, you may want to retouch your photos, run some software for your business, or play some new games. In each of these cases, you can search for an application, install it, and use it —usually, with no extra cost.

Software in Ubuntu is delivered as *packages*, making software installation a one-click, one-step process. A package is a compressed file archive containing everything needed to run the application. Packages can also contain other information, including the name of the packages which are required to run it. These packages, which are essential for the successful execution of other packages, are called *dependencies* or *libraries*. Linux is designed in a way so that any *library* can be updated without having to reinstall the complete application, minimizing hard drive usage by letting other applications use the same *library*.

Most other operating systems require a user to purchase commercial software (online or through a physical store), or search the Internet for a free alternative (if one is available). The correct installation file must then be verified for integrity, downloaded, and located on the computer, followed by the user proceeding through a number of installation prompts and options. By default, Ubuntu gives you a centralized point with two different ways to browse the *repositories* for searching, installing, and removing software.

- Ubuntu Software Center
- Command line apt-get

Searching, installing, and/or removing applications with Ubuntu Software Center is easy and convenient, and is the default application management system for both beginning and expert Ubuntu users.

Figure 5.1: Software Center icon
We recommend Ubuntu Software Center for searching, installing, and removing applications, although you still can use the command-line application apt-get, or install and use the advanced application Synaptic Package Manager.

Using the Ubuntu Software Center

There are numerous ways to install software on an operating system. In Ubuntu, the quickest and easiest way to find and install new applications is through the Ubuntu Software Center.

To start the application, click on the Ubuntu Software Center icon in the Launcher, or click on the Dash and search for Ubuntu Software Center.

The Ubuntu Software Center can be used to install applications available in the official Ubuntu repositories. The Software Center window has four sections—a list of categories on the left, a banner at the top, a Top Rated panel at the bottom, and a What's New and Recommended For You areas on the right. Clicking on a category will take you to a list of related applications. For example, the Internet category contains Firefox Web Browser. The featured areas highlight What's New and Top Rated software. Each area shows different application icons. Just click an icon to get more information

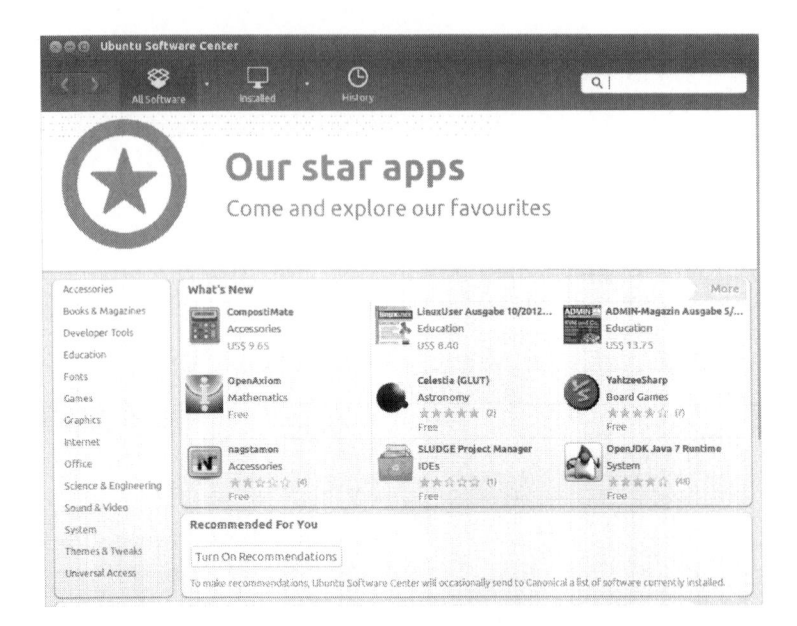

Figure 5.2: You can install and remove applications from your computer using the Software Center.

on the application or to install it. To see all software contained in the area, click **More**.

The three sections at the top represent your current view of the Software Center's catalog. Click the **All Software** button to see all installable software, click **Installed** to see a list of software that already installed on your computer, and click **History** to see previous installations and deletions organized by date.

Find your application

The Ubuntu Software Center displays different sources in the "Get Software" section. Clicking the arrow next to "All Software" will show a list of individual sections. Selecting "Provided by Ubuntu" will show free official software, "For Purchase" will show software for purchasing, and "Canonical Partners" will show software from partners of Canonical, such as Adobe.

If you are looking for an application, you may already know its specific name (for example, VLC Media Player), or you may just have a general category in mind (for example, the Sound and Video category includes a number of different software applications, such as video converters, audio editors, and music players).

To help you find the right application, you can browse the Software Center catalog by clicking on the category reflecting the type of software you seekr, or use the search field in the top right corner of the window to look for specific names or keywords.

When you select a category, you will be shown a list of applications. Some categories have sub-categories—for example, the Games category has subcategories for Simulation and Card Games. To move through categories, use the **back** and **forward** buttons at the top of the window.

Installing software

Once you have found an application you would like to try, installing it is just one click away.

To install software:

SOFTWARE MANAGEMENT 99

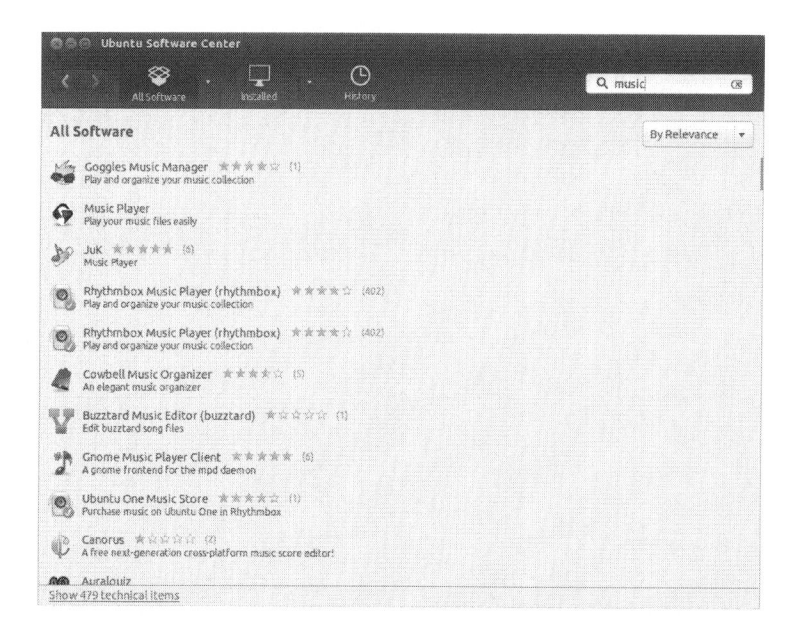

Figure 5.3: Searching for an application in the Ubuntu Software Center.

1. Click the **Install** button to the right of the selected package. If you would like to read more about the software package before installing it, first click on "More Info." This will take you to a short description of the application, as well as a screenshot and a web link when available. Related add-ons will be listed below the application's description. You can click **Install** from this screen as well. In addition, if you use the Gwibber micro-blogging application, you can click the "Share..." link below the description of an application to tell your friends about it.
2. After clicking **Install**, enter your password into the authentication window. This is the same password you use to log in to your account. You are required to enter your password whenever installing or removing software in order to prevent someone without administrator access from making unauthorized changes to your computer. If you receive an Authentication Failure message after typing in your password, check that you typed it correctly and try again.

You must have administrative privileges to install software, and you will need to be connected to the Internet and to the Software Center. To learn how to set up your Internet connection, see Getting online.

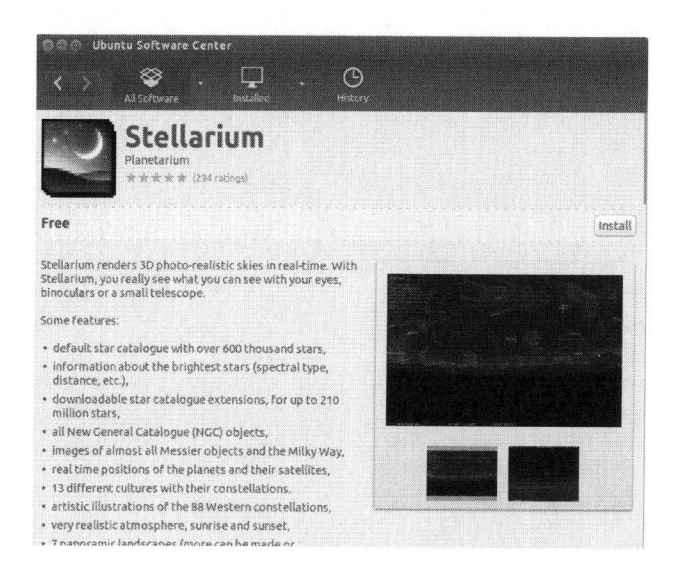

Figure 5.4: Here, clicking on "Install" will download and install the package "Stellarium."

3. Wait until the package is finished installing. During the installation (or

removal) of programs, you will see an animated icon of rotating arrows to the left of the **In Progress** button in the sidebar. If you like, you can now go back to the main browsing window and choose additional software packages to be installed by following the steps above. At any time, clicking the **Progress** button on the top will take you to a summary of all operations that are currently processing. You can also click the **X** icon to cancel any operation.

Once the Software Center has finished installing an application, it is ready to be used. You can start the newly installed application by going to the Dash and typing the name of the application in the search bar. By default application is added to the Launcher. You can change this behavior by deselecting **View ▸ New Applications in the Launcher**.

Removing software

Removing applications is very similar to installing them. First, find the installed software in the Ubuntu Software Center. You can click on the **Installed** button to see all installed software listed by categories. Scroll down to the application you wish to remove. If you click on the arrow next to the **Installed** button, you will find a list of software providers, which can help you narrow your search. You can also enter keywords into the Search field to quickly find installed software, or you can search by date in the History tab (more on History below).

Figure 5.5: Here, clicking on "Remove" will remove the package "SuperTux."

To remove software:

1. Click the **Remove** button to the right of the selected application.
2. Enter your password into the authentication window. Similar to installing software, removing software requires your password to help protect your computer against unauthorized changes. The package will then be queued for removal and will appear under the progress section at the top.

Removing a package will also update your menus accordingly.

Software history

The Ubuntu Software Center keeps track of past software management in the History section. This is useful if you wish to reinstall an application previously removed and do not remember the application's name.

There are four buttons in the history section—**All Changes**, **Installations**, **Updates**, and **Removals**. Clicking one will show a list of days the selected action occurred. If you click the arrow next to a day, a list of individual packages will be shown, along with what was done with them and at what time. The History section shows the history of all software installed on your computer, not just changes made within the Ubuntu Software Center. For example, packages updated through the software updater will also be listed.

Software Recommendations

The Ubuntu Software Center offers two types of recommendations—"per user" based and "per application" based. Click the **Turn On Recommendations** button in the right panel of the Ubuntu Software Center to enable per "user based" recommendations. You will have to log in with your Ubuntu Software Center account. This is the same as your Ubuntu One or Launchpad account. When you enable recommendations, the list of installed software will be periodically sent to servers of Canonical. Recommendations will appear in the same panel. If you want to disable these recommendations, go to **View ▸ Turn Off Recommendations**.

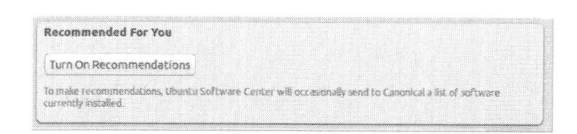

Figure 5.6: You can turn on Software Recommendations via clicking on the **Turn On Recommendations** button.

The "per application" based recommendations do not require log in. They are labeled as "People Also Installed." These are the applications installed by users who also installed the application which you are about to install. These recommendations are shown in the detailed page of the particular application.

Figure 5.7: The "People Also Installed" section shows applications installed by users who also installed the application which you are about to install.

Managing additional software

Although the Ubuntu Software Center provides a large library of applications from which to choose, only those packages available within the official Ubuntu repositories are listed. At times, you may be interested in a particular application not available in these repositories. If this happens, it is important to understand some alternative methods for accessing and installing software in Ubuntu, such as downloading an installation file manually from the Internet, or adding extra repositories. First, we will look at how to manage your repositories through Software Sources.

Software Sources

The Ubuntu Software Center lists only those applications that are available in your enabled repositories. Repositories can be added or removed through the Software Sources application. You can open Software Sources from the Ubuntu Software Center. Simply go to **Edit ▸ Software Sources** or open the HUD (Alt key) and search for "sources."

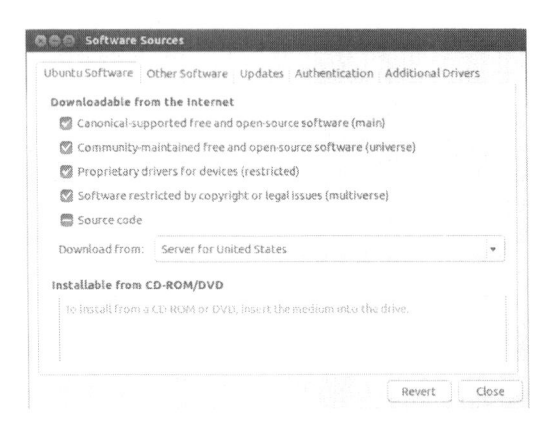

Figure 5.8: The Software Sources program enables you to add, remove and manage package repositories.

Managing the official repositories

When you open Software Sources, you will see the **Ubuntu Software** tab where the first four options are enabled by default.

The **Ubuntu Software** tab lists the official Ubuntu repositories, each containing different types of packages.

Canonical-supported open source software (main) This repository contains all the open-source packages maintained by Canonical.

Community-maintained open source software (universe) This repository contains all the open-source packages developed and maintained by the Ubuntu community.

Proprietary drivers for devices (restricted) This repository contains proprietary drivers which may be required to utilize the full capabilities of some of your devices or hardware.

Closed-source packages are sometimes referred to as *non-free*. This is a reference to freedom of speech, rather than monetary cost. Payment is not required to use these packages.

Software restricted by copyright or legal issues (multiverse) This repository contains software possibly protected from use in some states or countries by copyright or licensing laws. By using this repository, you assume responsibility for the usage of any packages that you install.

Source code This repository contains the source code used to build software packages from some of the other repositories. The **Source code**

Building applications from source is an advanced process for creating packages, and usually only concerns developers. You may also require source files when using a custom kernel, or if trying to use the latest version of an application before it is released for Ubuntu. As this is a more advanced area, it will not be covered in this manual.

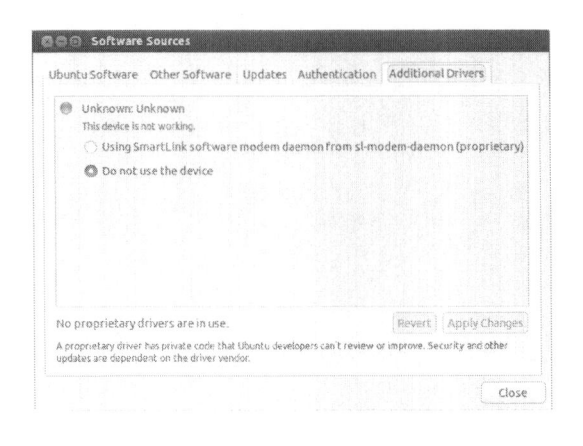

Figure 5.9: Drivers can be installed or removed via the Additional Drivers application.

option should not be selected unless you have experience with building applications from source.

Selecting the best software server

Ubuntu provides and allows many servers around the world to mirror the packages from the sources listed under "Managing the official repositories." When selecting a server, you may want to consider the following:

Distance to server. This will affect the speed you can achieve with the file server—the closer the server to your location, the faster the potential connection.

Internet Service Provider. Some Internet service providers offer low-cost or unlimited free downloads from their own servers.

Quality of server. Some servers may only offer downloads at a capped speed, limiting the rate at which you can install and update software on your computer.

Ubuntu will automatically choose an appropriate server while installing. It is recommended these settings not be changed unless your physical location significantly changes or if you feel a higher speed should be achieved by your Internet connection. The guide below will help in choosing an optimal server.

Ubuntu provides a tool for selecting the server that provides the fastest connection with your computer.

1. Click the dropdown box next to "Download from:" in the Software Sources window.
2. Select "Other..." from the list.
3. In the "Server Selection" window, click the **Select Best Server** button in the upper right. Your computer will now attempt a connection with all the available servers, then select the one with the fastest speed.

If you are happy with the automatic selection, click **Choose Server** to return to the Software Sources window.

If you are not happy with the automatic selection or prefer not to use the tool, the fastest server is often the closest server to you geographically. In this case, simply choose "Other" then find the nearest location to your location. When you are happy with the selection, click **Choose Server** to return to the Software Sources window.

If you do not have a working Internet connection, updates and programs can be installed from the installation media itself by inserting your media and clicking the box under "Installable from CD-ROM/DVD." Once this box is checked, the media within the CD-ROM/DVD drive will function as an online repository, and the software on the media will be installable from the Ubuntu Software Center.

Adding more software repositories

Ubuntu makes it easy to add additional, third-party repositories to your list of software sources. The most common repositories added to Ubuntu are called PPAs. PPAs allow you to install software packages that are not available in the official repositories and automatically be notified whenever updates for these packages are available.

Ubuntu grants permission to many servers all across the world to act as official *mirrors*. That is, they host an exact copy of all the files contained in the official Ubuntu repositories.

A PPA is a *Personal Package Archive*. These are online repositories used to host the latest versions of software packages, digital projects, and other applications.

If you know the web address of a PPA's Launchpad site, adding it to your list of software sources is relatively simple. To do so, you will need to use the **Other Software** tab in the "Software Sources" window.

On the Launchpad site for a PPA, you will see a heading to the left called "Adding this PPA to your system." Underneath will be a short paragraph containing a unique URL in the form of ppa:test-ppa/example. Highlight this URL by selecting it with your mouse, then right-click and select **Copy**.

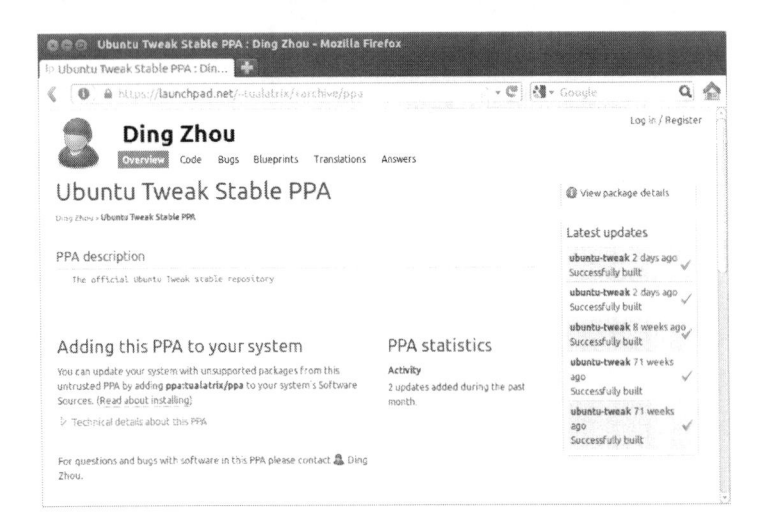

Figure 5.10: This is an example of the Launchpad page for the Ubuntu Tweak PPA. Ubuntu Tweak is an application that is not available in the official Ubuntu repositories. However, by adding this PPA to your list of software sources, it will be easy to install and update this application through the Software Center.

Return to the "Software Sources" window, and in the **Other Software** tab, click **Add...** at the bottom. A new window will appear, and you will see the words "Apt line:" followed by a text field. Right-click on the empty space in this text field and select **Paste**. You should see the URL appear you copied from the PPAs Launchpad site earlier. Click **Add Source** to return to the "Software Sources" window. You will see a new entry has been added to the list of sources in this window with a selected check box in front (meaning it is enabled).

If you click **Close** in the bottom right corner of this window, a message will appear informing you that "The information about available software is out-of-date." This is because you have just added a new repository to Ubuntu, and it now needs to connect to that repository and download a list of the packages it provides. Click **Reload**, and wait while Ubuntu refreshes all of your enabled repositories (including this new one you just added). When it has finished, the window will close automatically.

Congratulations, you have just added a PPA to your list of software sources. You can now open the Ubuntu Software Center and install applications from this PPA in the same way you previously installed applications from the default Ubuntu repositories.

Manual software installation

Although Ubuntu has extensive software available, you may want to manually install a software packages not available in the repositories. If no PPA exists for the software, you will need to install it manually. Before you choose to do so, make sure you trust the package and its maintainer.

Packages in Ubuntu have a `.deb` extension. Double-clicking a package will open an overview page in the Ubuntu Software Center, which will give you more information about that package.

The overview provides some technical information about that package, a website link (if applicable), and the option to install. Clicking **Install** will install the package just like any other installation in the Ubuntu Software Center.

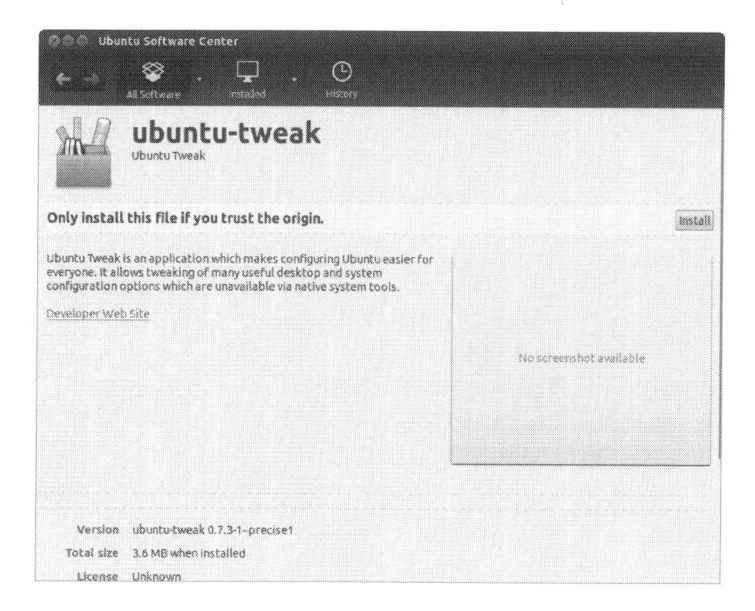

Figure 5.11: Installing .deb files manually using software center.

Updates and upgrades

Ubuntu also allows you to decide how to manage package updates through the **Updates** tab in the Software Sources window.

Ubuntu updates

In this section, you are able to specify the kinds of updates you wish to install on your system, and usually depends on your preferences around stability, versus having access to the latest developments.

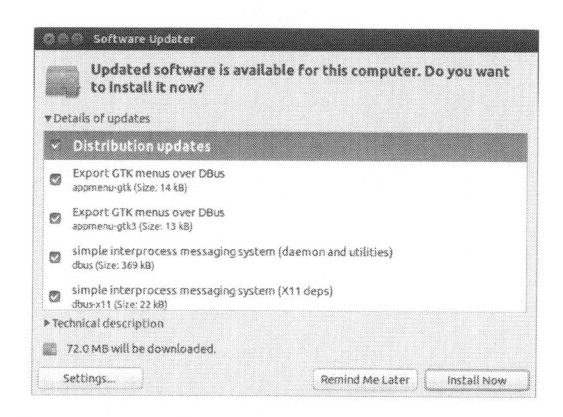

Figure 5.12: You can update installed software by using the Software Updater application in Ubuntu.

Important security updates These updates are highly recommended to ensure your system remains as secure as possible. These updates are enabled by default.

Recommended updates These updates are not as important in keeping your system secure. Rather, recommended updates will keep your software updated with the most recent bug fixes or minor updates that have been tested and approved. This option is also enabled by default.

Pre-released updates This option is for those who would rather remain up-to-date with the very latest releases of applications at the risk of installing an update that has unresolved bugs or conflicts. Note that it is possible you will encounter problems with these updated applications, therefore, this option is not enabled by default.

Unsupported updates These are updates that have not yet been fully tested and reviewed by Canonical. Some bugs may occur when using these updates, and so this option is also not enabled by default.

Automatic updates

The middle section of this window allows you to customize how your system manages updates, such as the frequency with which it checks for new packages, as well as whether it should install important updates right away (without asking for your permission), download them only, or just notify you about them.

Release upgrade

Here you can decide which system upgrades you would like to be notified about.

Never Choose this option if you would rather not be notified about any new Ubuntu releases.
For any new version Choose this option if you always want to have the latest Ubuntu release, regardless of whether it is a long-term support release or not. This option is recommended for normal home users.
For long-term support versions Choose this option if you need a release that will be more stable and have support for a longer time. If you use Ubuntu for business purposes, you may want to consider selecting this option.

Every six months, Canonical will release a new version of the Ubuntu operating system. These are called *normal releases*. Every four normal releases—or 24 months—Canonical releases a *long-term support* (LTS) release. Long-term support releases are intended to be the most stable releases available, and are supported for a longer period of time.

6 Advanced Topics

Ubuntu for advanced users

To this point, we've provided detailed instructions on getting the most from Ubuntu's basic features. In this chapter, we'll detail some of Ubuntu's more advanced features—like the terminal, a powerful utility that can help you accomplish tasks without the need for a graphical user interface (GUI). We'll also discuss some advanced security measures you can implement to make your computer even safer. We've written this chapter with advanced users in mind. If you're new to Ubuntu, don't feel as though you'll need to master these topics to get the most out of your new software (you can easily skip to the next chapter without any adverse impact to your experience with Ubuntu). However, if you're looking to expand your knowledge of Ubuntu, we encourage you to keep reading.

Introduction to the terminal

Throughout this manual, we have focused primarily on the graphical desktop user interface. In order to fully realize the power of Ubuntu, you will need to learn how to use the terminal.

What is the terminal?

Most operating systems, including Ubuntu, have two types of user interfaces. The first is a graphical user interface (GUI). This is the desktop, windows, menus, and toolbars you click to get things done. The second, much older type of interface is the command-line interface (CLI).

The *terminal* is Ubuntu's command-line interface. It is a method of controlling some aspects of Ubuntu using only commands that you type on the keyboard.

Why would I want to use the terminal?

You can perform most day-to-day activities without ever needing to open the terminal. However, the terminal is a powerful and invaluable tool that can be used to perform many useful tasks you might not be able to accomplish with a GUI. For example:

- Troubleshooting any difficulties that may arise when using Ubuntu sometimes requires you to use the terminal.
- A command-line interface is sometimes a faster way to accomplish a task. For example, it is often easier to perform operations on many files concurrently using the terminal.
- Learning the command-line interface is the first step towards more advanced troubleshooting, system administration, and software development skills. If you are interested in becoming a developer or an advanced Ubuntu user, knowledge of the command-line will be essential.

Opening the Terminal

You can open the terminal by clicking **Dash ‣ Applications ‣ Terminal**.

When the terminal window opens, it will be largely blank with the exception of some text at the top left of the screen, followed by a blinking block. This text is your prompt—it displays, by default, your login name and your computer's name, followed by the current directory. The tilde (~) means that the current directory is your home directory. Finally, the blinking block is called the cursor—this marks where text will be entered as you type.

To test a terminal command, type **pwd** and press Enter. The terminal should display /home/*yourusername*. This text is called the "output." You have just used the pwd (print working directory) command, which outputs (displays) the current directory.

> The *terminal* gives you access to what is called a *shell*. When you type a command in the terminal the shell interprets this command, resulting in the desired action. Different types of shells accept slightly different commands. The most popular is called "bash," and is the default shell in Ubuntu.

> In GUI environments the term "folder" is commonly used to describe a place where files are stored. In CLI environments the term "directory" is used to describe the same thing. This metaphor is exposed in many commands (*i.e.*, cd or pwd) throughout this chapter.

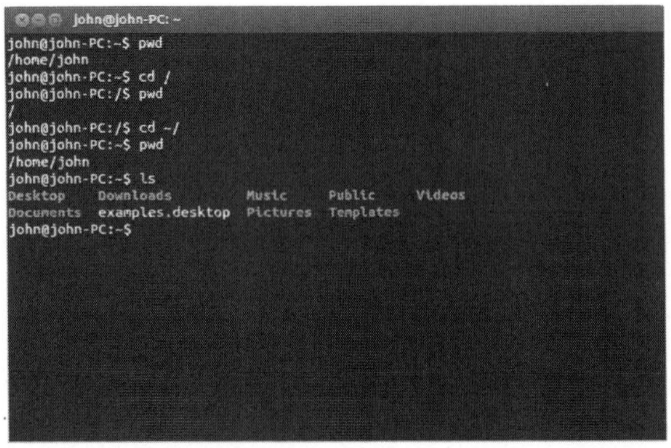

Figure 6.1: The default terminal window allows you to run hundreds of useful commands.

All commands in the terminal follow the same approach: Type a command, possibly followed by some parameters, and press Enter to perform the specified action. Often, some type of output will be displayed confirming the action was completed successfully, although this can depend on the command being executed. For example, using the cd command to change your current directory (see above) will change the prompt, but will not display any output.

The rest of this chapter covers some very common uses of the terminal. However, it cannot address the nearly infinite possibilities available to you when using the command-line interface in Ubuntu. Throughout the second part of this manual, we will continue to refer to the command line, particularly when discussing steps involved in troubleshooting as well as when describing more advanced management of your computer.

> *Parameters* are extra segments of text, usually added at the end of a command, that change how the command itself is interpreted. These usually take the form of **-h** or **--help**, for example. In fact, **--help** can be added to most commands to display a short description of the command, as well as a list of any other parameters that can be used with that command. Those adept in CLI experience will know these parameters by another name—switches.

Ubuntu file system structure

Ubuntu uses the Linux file system, which is based on a series of folders in the root directory. These folders contain important system files that cannot be modified unless you are running as the root user or use *sudo*. This restriction exists for both security and safety reasons: computer viruses will not be able to change the core system files, and ordinary users should not be able to accidentally damage anything vital.

We begin our discussion of the Ubuntu file system structure at the top, also known as the root directory—as denoted by /. The root directory contains all other directories and files on your system. Below the root directory are the following essential directories:

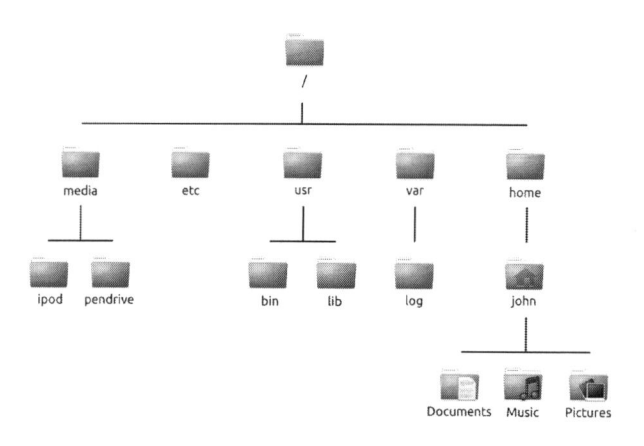

Figure 6.2: Some of the most important directories in the root file system.

/bin and /sbin Many essential system applications (equivalent to C:\Windows).
/etc System-wide configuration files.
/home Each user will have a subdirectory to store personal files (for example, /home/yourusername) which is equivalent to C:\Users or C:\Documents and Settings in Microsoft Windows.
/lib Library files, similar to .dll files on Windows.
/media Removable media (CD-ROMs and USB drives) will be mounted in this directory.
/root This contains the root user's files (not to be confused with the root directory).
/usr Pronounced "user," it contains most program files (not to be confused with each user's home directory). This is equivalent to C:\Program Files in Microsoft Windows.
/var/log Contains log files written by many applications.

Every directory has a *path*. The path is a directory's full name—it describes a way to navigate the directory from anywhere in the system.

For example, the directory /home/yourusername/Desktop contains all the files that are on your Ubuntu desktop. It can be broken down into a handful of key pieces:

- /—indicates that the path starts at the root directory
- home/—from the root directory, the path goes into the home directory
- yourusername/—from the home directory, the path goes into the yourusername directory
- Desktop—from the yourusername directory, the path ends up in the Desktop directory

Every directory in Ubuntu has a complete path that starts with the / (the root directory) and ends in the directory's own name.

Directories and files that begin with a period are hidden. These are usually only visible with a special command or by selecting a specific option. In Nautilus, you can show hidden files and directories by selecting **View ▸ Show Hidden Files**, or by pressing Ctrl+H. If you are using the terminal, then you would type `ls -a` and press Enter to see the hidden files and directories. There are many hidden directories in your home folder used to store program preferences. For example, /home/yourusername/.evolution stores preferences used by the Evolution mail application.

If you are creating a file or directory from the command line and ultimately want it hidden, then simply start the filename or directory name with a dot (.)—this signals to the filesystem that the file/directory should be hidden unless expressly viewed through showing hidden files and folders through the GUI or through the appropriate command line switch.

Mounting and unmounting removable devices

Any time you add storage media to your computer—an internal or external hard drive, a USB flash drive, a CD-ROM—it needs to be *mounted* before it is accessible. Mounting a device means to associate a directory name with the device, allowing you to navigate to the directory to access the device's files.

When a device, such as a USB flash drive or a media player, is mounted in Ubuntu, a folder is automatically created for it in the *media* directory, and you are given the appropriate permissions to be able to read and write to the device.

Most file managers will automatically add a shortcut to the mounted device in the side bar of your home folder or as a shortcut directly on the desktop so that so the device is easy to access. You shouldn't have to physically navigate to the *media* directory in Ubuntu, unless you choose to do so from the command line.

When you've finished using a device, you can *unmount* it. Unmounting a device disassociates the device from its directory, allowing you to eject it. If you disconnect or remove a storage device before unmounting it, you may lose data.

Securing Ubuntu

Now that you know a bit more about using the command line, we can use it to make your computer more secure. The following sections discuss various security concepts, along with procedures for keeping your Ubuntu running smoothly, safely, and securely.

Why Ubuntu is safe

Ubuntu is secure by default for a number of reasons:

- Ubuntu clearly distinguishes between normal users and administrative users.
- Software for Ubuntu is kept in a secure online repository, which contains no false or malicious software.
- Open-source software like Ubuntu allows security flaws to be easily detected.
- Security patches for open-source software like Ubuntu are often released quickly.
- Many viruses designed to primarily target Windows-based systems do not affect Ubuntu systems.

> Just because Ubuntu implements strong security by default doesn't mean the user can "throw caution to the wind." Care should be taken when downloading files, opening email, and browsing the Internet. Using a good antivirus program is warranted.

Basic security concepts

The following sections discuss basic security concepts—like file permissions, passwords, and user accounts. Understanding these concepts will help you in securing your computer.

Permissions

In Ubuntu, files and folders can be set up so that only specific users can view, modify, or run them. For instance, you might wish to share an important file with other users, but do not want those users to be able to edit the file. Ubuntu controls access to files on your computer through a system of "permissions." Permissions are settings configured to control exactly how files on your computer are accessed and used.

To learn more about modifying permissions, visit https://help.ubuntu.com/community/FilePermissions.

Passwords

You should use a strong password to increase the security of your computer. Your password should not contain names, common words, or common phrases. By default, the minimum length of a password in Ubuntu is four characters. We recommend a password with more than the minimum number of characters. A password with a minimum of eight characters which includes both upper and lower case letters, numbers, and symbols is considered strong.

Locking the screen

When you leave your computer unattended, you may want to lock the screen. Locking your screen prevents another user from using your computer until your password is entered. To lock the screen:

- Click the session menu icon in the right corner of the top panel, then select **Lock Screen**, or
- press Ctrl+Alt+L to lock the screen. This keyboard shortcut can be changed in **Dash ▸ Applications ▸ Keyboard Shortcuts**

User accounts

Users and groups

When Ubuntu is installed, it is automatically configured for use by a single user. If more than one person will use the computer, each person should have his or her own user account. This way, each user can have separate settings, documents, and other files. If necessary, you can also protect files from being viewed or modified by users without administrative privileges.

Like most operating systems, Ubuntu allows you to create separate user accounts for each person. Ubuntu also supports user groups, which allow you to administer permissions for multiple users at the same time.

Every user in Ubuntu is a member of at least one group—at a bare minimum, the user of the computer has permissions in a group with the same name as the user. A user can also be a member of additional groups. You can configure some files and folders to be accessible only by a user and a group. By default, a user's files are only accessible by that user; system files are only accessible by the root user.

Managing users

You can manage users and groups using the Users and Groups administration application. To find this application, click **Session Indicator ▸ Systems and Settings ▸ User Accounts**.

To adjust the user settings, first click the **Unlock** button and enter your password to unlock the user settings. Next, select the user that you want to modify from the list. Then click on the element that you want to change.

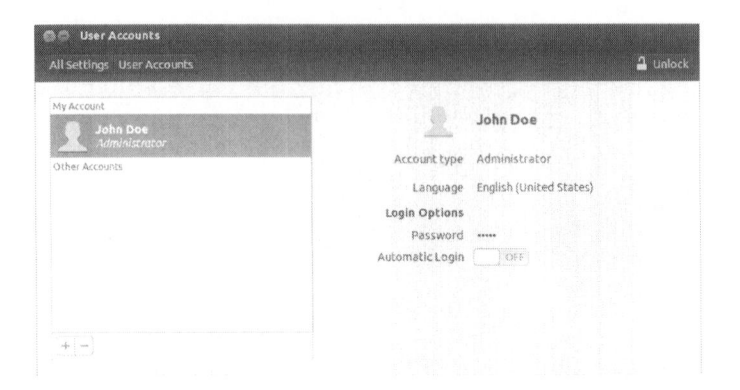

Figure 6.3: Add, remove and change the user accounts.

Adding a user Click the + button underneath the list of the current user accounts. A window will appear with two fields. The **Name** field contains a friendly display name. The **Username** field is for the actual username. Fill in the requested information, then click **OK**. A new dialog box will appear asking you to enter a password for the user you have just created. Fill out the fields, then click **OK**. You can also click the **gears** button to generate a password. Privileges you grant to the new user can be altered in "Users Settings".

Modifying a user Click on the name of a user in the list of users, then click on the text entry next to each of following options:

- Account type:
- Password:
- Automatic Login:

Deleting a user Select a user from the list and click -. Ubuntu will deactivate the user's account, and you can choose whether to remove the user's home folder or leave it in place. If a user is removed and the user's files remain, the only user who can access the files are the root user—also known as the superuser—or anyone associated with the file's group.

Managing groups

Group management is accomplished through the command line (Terminal) or by adding third-party applications (the latter is beyond the scope of this manual). You will find more information in the subsection "Using the command line" below.

Adding a group To add a group, type **sudo addgroup groupname** and press Enter, replacing *groupname* with the name of the group you wish to add.

Example: **sudo addgroup ubuntuusers**

Modifying a group To alter the users in an existing group, type **sudo adduser username groupname** (adding a user) or **sudo deluser username groupname** (removing a user) and press Enter, replacing *username* and *groupname* with the user and group name with which you're working.

Example: **sudo adduser jdoe ubuntuusers**
Example: **sudo deluser jdoe ubuntuusers**

Deleting a group To delete a group, type **sudo delgroup groupname** and press Enter, replacing *groupname* with the name of the group you wish to delete.

Example: **sudo delgroup ubuntuusers**

Applying groups to files and folders

To change the group associated with a file or folder, open the Nautilus file browser and navigate to the appropriate file or folder. Then, either select the folder and choose **File ▸ Properties** from the menu bar, or right-click on the file or folder and select **Properties**. In the Properties dialog window, click on the **Permissions** tab and select the desired group from the **Groups** drop-down list. Then close the window.

Using the command line

You can also modify user and group settings via the command line, but we recommend you use the graphical method above unless you have a good reason to use the command line. For more information on using the command line to modify users and groups, see the Ubuntu Server Guide at https://help.ubuntu.com/12.04/serverguide/C/user-management.html

System updates

Good security happens with an up-to-date system. Ubuntu provides free software and security updates. You should apply these updates regularly. See Updates and upgrades to learn how to update your Ubuntu computer with the latest security updates and patches.

Trusting third party sources

Normally, you will add applications to your computer via the Ubuntu Software Center which downloads software from the Ubuntu repositories as described in Chapter 5: Software Management. However, it is occasionally necessary to add software from other sources. For example, you may need to do this when an application is not available in the Ubuntu repositories or when you need a version of software newer than what is currently in the Ubuntu repositories.

Additional repositories are available from sites such as getdeb.net and Launchpad PPAs which can be added as described in Software Sources. You can download the DEB packages for some applications from their respective project sites on the Internet. Alternately, you can build applications from their source code (see margin note).

Using only recognized sources, such as a project's site, PPA, or various community repositories (such as getdeb.net) is more secure than downloading applications from an arbitrary (and perhaps less reputable) source. When using a third party source, consider its trustworthiness, and be sure you know exactly what you're installing on your computer.

> Source code is a term used to describe the code in which the application was written. Source code is readable by humans, but means nothing to the computer. Only when the source code is compiled will the computer know what to do with the source code).

Firewall

A firewall is an application that protects your computer against unauthorized access by people on the Internet or your local network. Firewalls block connections to your computer from unknown sources. This helps prevent security breaches.

Uncomplicated Firewall (UFW) is the standard firewall configuration program in Ubuntu. It runs from the command line, but a program called Gufw allows you to use it with a graphical user interface GUI. See Chapter 5: Software Management to learn more about installing the Gufw package.

Once Gufw is installed, start Gufw by clicking **Dash ▸ Applications ▸ Firewall configuration**. To enable the firewall, select the **Enable** option. By default, all incoming connections are denied. This setting should be suitable for most users.

If you are running server software on your Ubuntu system (such as a web server, or an FTP server), then you will need to open the ports these services use. If you are not familiar with servers, you will likely not need to open any additional ports.

To open a port click on the **Add** button. For most purposes, the **Preconfigured** tab is sufficient. Select **Allow** from the first box and then select the program or service required.

The **Simple** tab can be used to allow access on a single port, and the **Advanced** tab can be used to allow access on a range of ports.

Encryption

You may wish to protect your sensitive personal data—for instance, financial records—by encrypting it. Encrypting a file or folder essentially "locks" that file or folder by encoding it with an algorithm that keeps it scrambled until it is properly decoded with a password. Encrypting your personal data ensures that no one can open your personal folders or read your private data without your authorization through the use of a private key.

Ubuntu includes a number of tools to encrypt files and folders. This chapter will discuss two of them. For further information on using encryption with either single files or email, see Ubuntu Community Help documents at https://help.ubuntu.com/community.

Home folder

When installing Ubuntu, it is possible to encrypt a user's home folder. See Chapter 1: Installation for more on encrypting the home folder.

Private folder

If you have not chosen to encrypt a user's entire home folder, it is possible to encrypt a single folder—called `Private`—in a user's home folder. To do this, follow these steps:

1. Install the `ecryptfs-utils` software package from the Ubuntu Software Center. (For more information about the Software Center, review Using the Ubuntu Software Center.)
2. Use the terminal to run `ecryptfs-setup-private` to set up the private folder.
3. Enter your account's password when prompted.
4. Either choose a mount passphrase or generate one.
5. Record both passphrases in a safe location. *These are required if you ever have to recover your data manually.*
6. Log out and log back in to mount the encrypted folder.

After the `Private` folder has been set up, any files or folders in it will automatically be encrypted.

If you need to recover your encrypted files manually see https://help.ubuntu.com/community/EncryptedPrivateDirectory.

7 Troubleshooting

Resolving problems

Sometimes things may not work as they should. Luckily, problems encountered while working with Ubuntu are often easily fixed. This chapter is meant as a guide for resolving basic problems users may encounter while using Ubuntu. If you need any additional help beyond what is provided in this chapter, take a look at other support options that are discussed in Finding additional help and support later in this book.

Troubleshooting guide

The key to effective troubleshooting is to work slowly, complete all of troubleshooting steps, and to document the changes you made to the utility or application you are using. This way, you will be able to undo your work, or give fellow users the information about your previous attempts—the latter is particularly helpful in cases when you look to the community of Ubuntu users for support.

Ubuntu fails to start after I've installed Windows

Occasionally you may install Ubuntu and then decide to install Microsoft Windows as a second operating system running side-by-side with Ubuntu. This is supported in Ubuntu, but you might also find after installing Windows that you will no longer be able to start Ubuntu.

When you first turn on your computer, a "bootloader" is responsible for initiating the start of an operating system, such as Ubuntu or Windows. When you installed Ubuntu, you automatically installed an advanced bootloader called GRUB. GRUB allows you to choose between the various operating systems installed on your computer, such as Ubuntu, Windows, Solaris, or Mac OS X. If Ubuntu was installed first, then Windows was installed, the Windows installation removed GRUB and replaced the bootloader with it's own. As a result, you can no longer choose an operating system to use. You can restore GRUB and regain the ability to choose your operating system by following the steps below, using the same DVD you used to install Ubuntu.

A *bootloader* is the initial software that loads the operating system when the computer is powered up.

First, insert your Ubuntu DVD into your computer and then restart the computer, making sure to instruct your computer to boot from the DVD drive and not the hard drive (see Chapter 1: Installation). Next, choose your language (*e.g.*, English) and select **Try Ubuntu**. Once Ubuntu starts, click on the top-most icon in the Launcher (the Dash icon). Then, search for **Terminal** using the search box. Then, select Terminal in the search results. A window should open with a blinking prompt line. Enter the following, and press the Enter key:

```
$ sudo fdisk -l
Disk /dev/hda: 120.0 GB, 120034123776 bytes
255 heads, 63 sectors/track, 14593 cylinders
Units = cylinders of 16065 * 512 = 8225280 bytes

   Device Boot      Start         End      Blocks   Id  System
/dev/sda1               1        1224       64228+  83  Linux
```

```
/dev/sda2    *    1225    2440    9767520    a5  Windows
/dev/sda3         2441   14593   97618972+    5  Extended
/dev/sda4        14532   14593     498015    82  Linux swap

Partition table entries are not in disk order
```

This output shows that your system (Linux, on which Ubuntu is based) is installed on device `/dev/sda1`, but as indicated by the asterisk in the Boot column, your computer is booting to `/dev/sda2` (where Windows is located). We need to fix this by telling the computer to boot to the Linux device instead.

To do this, create a place to connect your existing Ubuntu installation with your temporary troubleshooting session:

```
$ sudo mkdir /media/root
```

Next, link your Ubuntu installation and this new folder:

```
$ sudo mount /dev/sda1 /media/root
```

If you've done this correctly, then you should see the following:

```
$ ls /media/root
bin dev home lib mnt root srv usr
boot etc initrd lib64 opt sbin sys var
cdrom initrd.img media proc selinux tmp vmlinuz
```

Now, you can reinstall GRUB:

```
$ sudo grub-install --root-directory=/media/root /dev/sda
Installation finished. No error reported.
This is the contents of the device map /boot/grub/device.map.
Check if this is correct or not. If any of the lines is incorrect,
fix it and re-run the script grub-install.
(hd0) /dev/sda
```

Finally, remove the Ubuntu disc from your DVD-ROM drive, reboot your computer, and then start enjoying your Ubuntu operating system once again.

This guide may not work for all Ubuntu users due to differences in the various system configuration. Still, this is the recommended and most successful method for restoring the GRUB bootloader. If you are following this guide and if it does not restore GRUB on your computer, then try the other troubleshooting methods at https://help.ubuntu.com/community/RecoveringUbuntuAfterInstallingWindows.

I forgot my password

If you forgot your password in Ubuntu, you will need to reset it using the "Recovery mode."

To start the Recovery mode, shut down your computer and then start again. As the computer starts up, press Shift. Select the **Recovery mode** option using the arrow keys on your keyboard. Recovery mode should be the second item in the list.

Wait until Ubuntu starts up—this may take a few minutes. Once booted, you *will not* be able to see a normal login screen. Instead, you will be presented with the **Recovery Menu**. Select **root** using the arrow keys and press Enter.

You will now be at a terminal prompt:

> The device (/dev/sda1, /dev/sda2, etc.) we are looking for is identified by the word "Linux" in the System column. Modify the instructions below if necessary, replacing /dev/sda1 with the name of your Linux device.

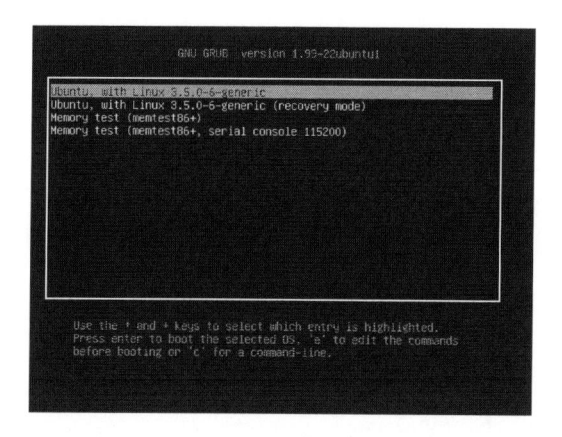

Figure 7.1: This is the grub screen in which you can choose recovery mode.

root@ubuntu:~#

To reset your password, enter:

`# passwd `*`username`*

Replace "username" above with your username, after which Ubuntu will prompt you for a new password. Enter your desired password, press the Enter key, and then re-type your password again, pressing the Enter again when done. (Ubuntu asks for your password twice to make sure you did not make a mistake while typing). Once you have restored your password, return to the normal system environment by entering:

`# init 2`

Login as usual and continue enjoying Ubuntu.

I accidentally deleted some files that I need

If you've deleted a file by accident, you may be able to recover it from Ubuntu's Trash folder. This is a special folder where Ubuntu stores deleted files before they are permanently removed from your computer.

To access the Trash folder click on the trash icon at the bottom of the Unity Launcher.

If you want to restore deleted items from the Trash:

1. Open Trash
2. Click on each item you want to restore to select it. Press and hold `Ctrl` to select multiple items.
3. Click **Restore Selected Items** to move the deleted items back to their original locations.

How do I clean Ubuntu?

Ubuntu's software packaging system accumulates unused packages and temporary files through regular updates and use. These temporary files, also called caches, contain files from all of the installed packages. Over time, this cache can grow quite large. Cleaning out the cache allows you to reclaim space on your computer's hard drive for storing your documents, music, photographs, or other files.

To clear the cache, you can either use the `clean`, or the `autoclean` option for the command-line program `apt-get`.

To run `clean`, open Terminal and enter:

```
$ sudo apt-get clean
```

Packages can also become unused over time. If a package was installed to assist with running another program—and that program was subsequently removed—you no longer need the supporting package. You can remove it with `apt-get autoremove`.

Load Terminal and enter:

```
$ sudo apt-get autoremove
```

> The `clean` command will remove every single cached item, while the `autoclean` command only removes cached items that can no longer be downloaded (these items are often unnecessary).

I can't play certain audio or video files

Many of the formats used to deliver rich media content are *proprietary*, meaning they are not free to use, modify, or distribute with an open-source operating system like Ubuntu. Therefore, Ubuntu does not include the capability to use these formats by default; however, users can easily configure Ubuntu to use these proprietary formats. For more information about the differences between open source and proprietary software, see Chapter 8: Learning More.

If you find yourself in need of a proprietary format, you can install the required files from the Ubuntu Software Center. Ensure that you have Universe and Multiverse repositories enabled before continuing. See the Software Sources section to learn how to enable these repositories. When you are ready to continue, install the necessary software as follows:

1. Open the Ubuntu Software Center by searching for it from the Dash (the top-most button on the Launcher).
2. Search for `ubuntu-restricted-extras` by typing "Ubuntu restricted extras" in the search box on the right-hand side of the Ubuntu Software Center main window. When the Software Center finds the appropriate software, click the arrow next to its title.
3. Click **Install**, then wait while Ubuntu installs the software.

One program that can play many of these formats is VLC media player. It can be installed from the Ubuntu Software Center. Once Ubuntu has successfully installed this software, your rich media content should work properly.

How can I change my screen resolution?

The image on every monitor is composed of millions of little colored dots called pixels. Changing the number of pixels displayed on your monitor is called "changing the resolution." Increasing the resolution will make the displayed images sharper, but will also tend to make them smaller. The opposite is true when screen resolution is decreased. Most monitors have a "native resolution," which is a resolution that most closely matches the number of pixels in the monitor. Your display will usually be sharpest when your operating system uses a resolution that matches your display's native resolution.

The Ubuntu configuration utility Displays allows users to change the resolution. Open it by clicking on the **session indicator** and then on **Displays…**. The resolution can be changed using the drop-down list within the program. Picking options higher up on the list (for example, those with larger numbers) will increase the resolution.

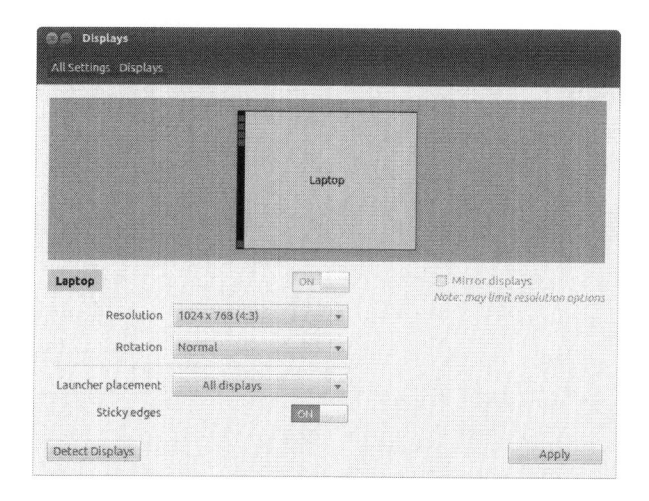

Figure 7.2: You can change your display settings.

You can experiment with various resolutions by clicking **Apply** at the bottom of the window until you find one that is comfortable. Typically, the highest resolution will be the native resolution. Selecting a resolution and clicking **Apply** will temporarily change the screen resolution to the selected value, and a dialog box will also be displayed for 30 seconds. This dialog box allows you to revert to the previous resolution setting or keep the new resolution setting. If you've not accepted the new resolution and/or 30 seconds have passed, the dialog box will disappear and the display's resolution will return to its previous setting.

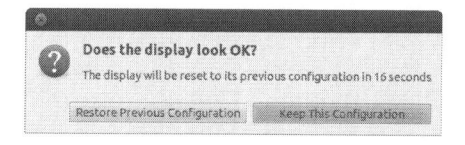

Figure 7.3: You can revert back to your old settings if you need to.

This feature was implemented to prevent someone from being locked out of the computer by a resolution that distorts the monitor output and makes it unusable. When you have finished setting the screen resolution, click **Close**.

Ubuntu is not working properly on my Apple MacBook or MacBook Pro

When installed on notebook computers from Apple—such as the MacBook or MacBook Pro—Ubuntu does not always enable all of the computer's built-in components, including the iSight camera and the Airport wireless Internet adapter. Luckily, the Ubuntu community offers documentation on fixing these and other problems. If you are having trouble installing or using Ubuntu on your Apple notebook computer, please follow the instructions at https://help.ubuntu.com/community/MacBook. You can select the appropriate guide after identifying your computer's model number.

Ubuntu is not working properly on my Asus EeePC

When installed on netbook computers from Asus—such as the EeePC— Ubuntu does not always enable all of the computer's built-in components, including the keyboard shortcut keys and the wireless Internet adapter. The Ubuntu community offers documentation on enabling these components and fixing other problems. If you are having trouble installing or using Ubuntu on your Asus EeePC, please follow the instructions at https://help.ubuntu.com/community/EeePC. This documentation page contains information pertaining specifically to EeePC netbooks.

To enable many of the features and Function Keys, a quick fix is to add "acpi_osi=Linux" to your grub configuration. From the Terminal

```
$ gksudo gedit /etc/default/grub
```

and very carefully change the line

```
GRUB_CMDLINE_LINUX_DEFAULT="quiet splash"
```

to

```
GRUB_CMDLINE_LINUX_DEFAULT="quiet splash acpi_osi=Linux"
```

Save and close the file. Then, from the terminal:

```
sudo update-grub
```

After the command finishes, and you restart the computer, you will be able to use the Fn keys normally.

My hardware is not working properly

Ubuntu occasionally has difficulty running on certain computers, usually when hardware manufacturers use non-standard or proprietary components. The Ubuntu community offers documentation to help you troubleshoot many common issues in this situation, including problems with wireless cards, scanners, mice, and printers. You can find the complete hardware troubleshooting guide on Ubuntu's support wiki, accessible at https://wiki.ubuntu.com/HardwareSupport. If your hardware problems persist, please see Getting more help for more troubleshooting options or information on obtaining support or assistance from an Ubuntu user.

Getting more help

This guide does not cover every possible workflow, task, issue, or problem in Ubuntu. If you require assistance beyond the information in the manual, you can find a variety of support opportunities online.

More details about many support options available to you can be found at Finding additional help and support later in this book.

8 Learning More

What else can I do with Ubuntu?

You should now be able to use Ubuntu for most of your daily activities —such as browsing the web, sending email, and creating documents. But you may be interested in learning about other versions of Ubuntu you can integrate into your digital lifestyle. In this chapter, we'll introduce you to additional versions of Ubuntu specialized for certain tasks. We'll also provide you with resources for answering any remaining questions you may have, and tell you how you can get involved in the worldwide community of Ubuntu users. But first, we'll discuss the technologies that make Ubuntu a powerful collection of software.

Open source software

Ubuntu is open source software. Open source software differs from proprietary software—software whose source code is not freely available for modification or distribution by anyone but the rightsholder. Microsoft Windows and Adobe Photoshop are examples of proprietary software.

Unlike proprietary software applications, the software included with Ubuntu is specifically licensed to promote sharing and collaboration. The legal rules governing Ubuntu's production and distribution ensure that anyone can obtain, run, or share it for any purpose she or he wishes. Computer users can modify open source software like Ubuntu to suit their individual needs, to share it, to improve it, or to translate it into other languages—provided they release the source code for these modifications so others can do the same. In fact, the terms of many open source licensing agreements actually make it illegal not to do so. For more information regarding Ubuntu's software licensing standards, see http://www.ubuntu.com/project/about-ubuntu/licensing.

Because open source software is developed by large communities of programmers distributed throughout the globe, it benefits from rapid development cycles and speedy security releases (in the event that someone discovers bugs in the software). In other words, open source software is updated, enhanced, and made more secure every day as programmers all over the world continue to improve it.

Aside from these technical advantages, open source software also has economic benefits. While users must adhere to the terms of an open source licensing agreement when installing and using Ubuntu, they needn't pay to obtain this license. And while not all open source software is free of monetary costs, much is.

To learn more about open source software, see the Open Source Initiative's open source definition, available at http://www.opensource.org/docs/definition.php.

Distribution families

Ubuntu is one of several popular operating systems based on Linux (an open source operating system). These Linux-based operating systems—

> The *source code* of a program is the collection of files that have been written in a computer language to make the program.
>
> *Proprietary software* is software that cannot be copied, modified, or distributed freely.

called Linux "distributions,"—may look different from Ubuntu at first glance, but they share similar characteristics because of their common roots.

Linux distributions can be divided into two broad families: the Debian family and the Red Hat family. Each family is named for a distribution on which subsequent distributions are based. For example, "Debian" refers to both the name of a Linux distribution as well as the family of distributions derived from Debian. Ubuntu is part of this family. When describing relationships between various open source projects, software developers often use the metaphor of tributaries connecting to a common body of water. For this reason, you may hear someone say that Ubuntu is located "downstream" from Debian, because alterations to Debian flow into new versions of Ubuntu. Additionally, improvements to Ubuntu usually trickle "upstream"—back to Debian and its family members, which benefit from the work of the Ubuntu community. Other distributions in the Debian family include Linux Mint, Xandros, and CrunchBang Linux. Distributions in the Red Hat family include Fedora, and Mandriva.

The most significant difference between Debian-based and Red Hat-based distributions is the system each uses for installing and updating software. These systems are called "package management systems." Debian software packages are DEB files, while Red Hat software packages are RPM files. The two systems are generally incompatible. For more information about package management, see Chapter 5: Software Management.

Package management systems are the means by which users can install, remove, and organize software installed on computers with open source operating systems like Ubuntu.

You will also find Linux distributions that have been specialized for certain tasks. Next, we'll describe these versions of Ubuntu and explain the uses for which each has been developed.

Choosing amongst Ubuntu and its derivatives

Just as Ubuntu is based on Debian, several distributions are subsequently based on Ubuntu. Each differs with respect to the software included as part of the distribution. Some are developed for general use, while others are designed for accomplishing a more narrow set of tasks.

Alternative interfaces

Ubuntu features a graphical user interface (GUI) based on the open source GNOME desktop. As we explained in Chapter 2: The Ubuntu Desktop, a "user interface" is a collection of software elements—icons, colors, windows, themes, and menus—that determines how someone may interact with a computer. Some people prefer using alternatives to GNOME, so they have created Ubuntu distributions featuring different user interfaces. These include:

- Kubuntu, which uses the KDE graphical environment instead of the GNOME environment found in Ubuntu;
- Lubuntu, which uses the LXDE graphical environment instead of the GNOME environment found in Ubuntu; and
- Xubuntu, which uses the XFCE graphical environment instead of the GNOME environment found in Ubuntu.

Additionally, each of these distributions may contain default applications different from those featured in Ubuntu. For instance, the default music player in Ubuntu is Rhythmbox, but in Lubuntu the default music player is Aqualung, and in Kubuntu the default is Amarok. Be sure to investigate these differences if you are considering installing an Ubuntu distribution with an alternative desktop environment.

For more information about these and other derivative distributions, see http://www.ubuntu.com/project/derivatives.

Task-specific distributions

Other Ubuntu distributions have been created to accomplish specific tasks or run in specialized settings.

Ubuntu Server Edition

The Ubuntu Server Edition is an operating system optimized to perform multi-user tasks when installed on servers. Such tasks include file sharing and website or email hosting. If you are planning to use a computer to perform tasks like these, you may wish to use this specialized server distribution in conjunction with server hardware.

This manual does not explain the process of running a secure web server or performing other tasks possible with Ubuntu Server Edition. For details on using Ubuntu Server Edition, refer to the manual at http://www.ubuntu.com/business/server/overview.

Edubuntu

Edubuntu is an Ubuntu derivative customized for use in schools and other educational institutions. It contains software similar to that offered in Ubuntu, but also features additional applications—like a collaborative text editor and educational games.

For additional information regarding Edubuntu, visit http://www.edubuntu.org/

Ubuntu Studio

This derivative of Ubuntu is designed specifically for people who use computers to create and edit multimedia projects. It features applications to help users manipulate images, compose music, and edit video. While users can install these applications on computers running the desktop version of Ubuntu, Ubuntu Studio makes them all available immediately upon installation.

If you would like to learn more about Ubuntu Studio (or obtain a copy for yourself), visit http://ubuntustudio.org/home.

Mythbuntu

Mythbuntu allows users to turn their computers into entertainment systems. It helps users organize and view various types of multimedia content such as movies, television shows, and video podcasts. Users with TV tuners in their computers can also use Mythbuntu to record live video and television shows.

To learn more about Mythbuntu, visit http://www.mythbuntu.org/.

Finding additional help and support

This guide cannot possibly contain everything you'll ever need to know about Ubuntu. We encourage you to take advantage of Ubuntu's vast community when seeking further information, troubleshooting technical issues, or asking questions about your computer. Next, we'll discuss a few of these resources so you can learn more about Ubuntu or other Linux distributions.

Live chat

If you are familiar with Internet relay chat (IRC), you can use chat clients such as XChat or Pidgin to join the channel #ubuntu on irc.freenode.net. Here, hundreds of volunteer users can answer your questions or offer support in real time. To learn more about using Internet Relay Chat to seek help with Ubuntu, visit https://help.ubuntu.com/community/InternetRelayChat.

LoCo teams

Within the Ubuntu community are dozens of local user groups called "LoCo teams." Spread throughout the world, these teams offer support and advice, answer questions and promote Ubuntu in their communities by hosting regular events. To locate and contact the LoCo team nearest you, visit http://loco.ubuntu.com/.

Books and Magazines

Many books have been written about Ubuntu, and professional magazines often feature news and information related to Ubuntu. You will frequently find these resources at your local bookstore or newsstand. However, many of these print publications are also available as digital downloads for purchase in the Ubuntu Software Center. To find these, launch the Software Center, then click on "Books & Magazines" in the left panel.

Official Ubuntu Documentation

The Ubuntu Documentation team maintains a series of official wiki pages designed to assist both new and experienced users wishing to learn more about Ubuntu. The Ubuntu community endorses these documents, which serve as a reliable first point of reference for users seeking help online. You can access these at http://help.ubuntu.com. To get to the built-in Ubuntu Desktop Guide, press F1 on your desktop, or type yelp in the Dash.

In addition to official Ubuntu and community help, you will often find third-party help available on the Internet. While these documents can often seem like great resources, some could be misleading or outdated. It's always best to verify information from third-party sources before taking their advice. When possible, rely on official Ubuntu documentation for assistance with Ubuntu.

The Ubuntu Forums

The Ubuntu Forums are the official forums of the Ubuntu community. Millions of Ubuntu users use them daily to seek help and support from one another. You can create an Ubuntu Forums account in minutes. To create an account and learn more about Ubuntu from community members, visit http://ubuntuforums.org.

Launchpad Answers

Launchpad, an open source code repository and user community, provides a question and answer service that allows anyone to ask questions about any Ubuntu-related topic. Signing up for a Launchpad account requires only a few minutes. You can ask a question by visiting Launchpad at https://answers.launchpad.net/ubuntu/+addquestion.

Ask Ubuntu

Ask Ubuntu is a free, community-driven website for Ubuntu users and developers. Like the Ubuntu Forums, it allows users to post questions that other members of the Ubuntu community can answer. But Ask Ubuntu also allows visitors to "vote" on the answers users provide, so the most useful or helpful responses get featured more prominently on the site. Ask ubuntu is part of the Stack Exchange network of websites, and is one of the best Ubuntu support resources available at no cost. Visit http://www.askubuntu.com to get started.

Search Engines

Because Ubuntu is a popular open source operating system, many users have written about it online. Therefore, using search engines to locate answers to your questions about Ubuntu is often an effective means of acquiring help. When using search engines to answer questions about Ubuntu, ensure that your search queries are as specific as possible. In other words, a search for "Unity interface" will return results that are less useful than those associated with the query "how to use Ubuntu Unity interface" or "how to customize Ubuntu Unity interface."

Community support

If you've exhausted all these resources and still can't find answers to your questions, visit Community Support at http://www.ubuntu.com/support/community.

The Ubuntu community

Surrounding Ubuntu is a global community of passionate users who want to help others adopt, use, understand, and even modify or enhance Ubuntu. By choosing to install and run Ubuntu, you've become part of this community. As you learn more about Ubuntu, you may wish to collaborate with others to make it better—to discuss the future of Ubuntu, to report software bugs you discover, to promote Ubuntu to new users, to share Ubuntu advice, or to answer other users' questions. In this section, we'll discuss a few community projects that can connect you to other Ubuntu users.

Full Circle Magazine

Full Circle Magazine is "the independent magazine for the Ubuntu Linux community." Released every month, Full Circle Magazine contains reviews of new software (including games) for Ubuntu, step-by-step tutorials for projects you can undertake with Ubuntu, editorials discussing important issues in the Ubuntu community, and Ubuntu tips from other users. You can download issues of Full Circle Magazine at http://fullcirclemagazine.org/.

The Ubuntu UK Podcast

Produced by members of the UK's Ubuntu LoCo team, this bi-weekly online audio broadcast (or "podcast") features lively discussion about Ubuntu, and often includes interviews with Ubuntu community members who work to improve Ubuntu. Episodes are available at http://podcast.ubuntu-uk.org/.

A *podcast* is a radio-style broadcast available as an audio file for download to computers and portable media players.

OMG! Ubuntu!

OMG! Ubuntu! is a weblog that aims to inform the Ubuntu community about Ubuntu news, events, announcements, and updates in a timely fashion. It also allows Ubuntu users to discuss ways they can promote or share Ubuntu. You can read this blog or subscribe to it at http://www.omgubuntu.co.uk/.

Contributing

Contributing to Ubuntu

As we mentioned earlier in this chapter, Ubuntu is a community-maintained operating system. You can help make Ubuntu better in a number of ways. The community consists of thousands of individuals and teams. If you would like to contribute to Ubuntu, please visit https://wiki.ubuntu.com/ContributeToUbuntu.

You can also participate in the Ubuntu community by contributing to this manual. You might choose to write new content for it, edit its chapters so they are easier for new Ubuntu users to understand and use, or translate it in your own language. You may also provide the screenshots found throughout the manual. To get involved in the Ubuntu Manual Project, visit http://ubuntu-manual.org/getinvolved.

A License

Creative Commons Attribution–ShareAlike 3.0 Legal Code

THE WORK (AS DEFINED BELOW) IS PROVIDED UNDER THE TERMS OF THIS CREATIVE COMMONS PUBLIC LICENSE ("CCPL" OR "LICENSE"). THE WORK IS PROTECTED BY COPYRIGHT AND/OR OTHER APPLICABLE LAW. ANY USE OF THE WORK OTHER THAN AS AUTHORIZED UNDER THIS LICENSE OR COPYRIGHT LAW IS PROHIBITED.

BY EXERCISING ANY RIGHTS TO THE WORK PROVIDED HERE, YOU ACCEPT AND AGREE TO BE BOUND BY THE TERMS OF THIS LICENSE. TO THE EXTENT THIS LICENSE MAY BE CONSIDERED TO BE A CONTRACT, THE LICENSOR GRANTS YOU THE RIGHTS CONTAINED HERE IN CONSIDERATION OF YOUR ACCEPTANCE OF SUCH TERMS AND CONDITIONS.

1. Definitions
    (a) "Adaptation" means a work based upon the Work, or upon the Work and other pre-existing works, such as a translation, adaptation, derivative work, arrangement of music or other alterations of a literary or artistic work, or phonogram or performance and includes cinematographic adaptations or any other form in which the Work may be recast, transformed, or adapted including in any form recognizably derived from the original, except that a work that constitutes a Collection will not be considered an Adaptation for the purpose of this License. For the avoidance of doubt, where the Work is a musical work, performance or phonogram, the synchronization of the Work in timed-relation with a moving image ("synching") will be considered an Adaptation for the purpose of this License.
    (b) "Collection" means a collection of literary or artistic works, such as encyclopedias and anthologies, or performances, phonograms or broadcasts, or other works or subject matter other than works listed in Section 1(f) below, which, by reason of the selection and arrangement of their contents, constitute intellectual creations, in which the Work is included in its entirety in unmodified form along with one or more other contributions, each constituting separate and independent works in themselves, which together are assembled into a collective whole. A work that constitutes a Collection will not be considered an Adaptation (as defined below) for the purposes of this License.
    (c) "Creative Commons Compatible License" means a license that is listed at http://creativecommons.org/compatiblelicenses that has been approved by Creative Commons as being essentially equivalent to this License, including, at a minimum, because that license: (i) contains terms that have the same purpose, meaning and effect as the License Elements of this License; and, (ii) explicitly permits the relicensing of adaptations of works made available under that license under this License or a Creative Commons jurisdiction license with the same License Elements as this License.
    (d) "Distribute" means to make available to the public the original and copies of the Work or Adaptation, as appropriate, through sale or other transfer of ownership.

(e) "License Elements" means the following high-level license attributes as selected by Licensor and indicated in the title of this License: Attribution, ShareAlike.

(f) "Licensor" means the individual, individuals, entity or entities that offer(s) the Work under the terms of this License.

(g) "Original Author" means, in the case of a literary or artistic work, the individual, individuals, entity or entities who created the Work or if no individual or entity can be identified, the publisher; and in addition (i) in the case of a performance the actors, singers, musicians, dancers, and other persons who act, sing, deliver, declaim, play in, interpret or otherwise perform literary or artistic works or expressions of folklore; (ii) in the case of a phonogram the producer being the person or legal entity who first fixes the sounds of a performance or other sounds; and, (iii) in the case of broadcasts, the organization that transmits the broadcast.

(h) "Work" means the literary and/or artistic work offered under the terms of this License including without limitation any production in the literary, scientific and artistic domain, whatever may be the mode or form of its expression including digital form, such as a book, pamphlet and other writing; a lecture, address, sermon or other work of the same nature; a dramatic or dramatico-musical work; a choreographic work or entertainment in dumb show; a musical composition with or without words; a cinematographic work to which are assimilated works expressed by a process analogous to cinematography; a work of drawing, painting, architecture, sculpture, engraving or lithography; a photographic work to which are assimilated works expressed by a process analogous to photography; a work of applied art; an illustration, map, plan, sketch or three-dimensional work relative to geography, topography, architecture or science; a performance; a broadcast; a phonogram; a compilation of data to the extent it is protected as a copyrightable work; or a work performed by a variety or circus performer to the extent it is not otherwise considered a literary or artistic work.

(i) "You" means an individual or entity exercising rights under this License who has not previously violated the terms of this License with respect to the Work, or who has received express permission from the Licensor to exercise rights under this License despite a previous violation.

(j) "Publicly Perform" means to perform public recitations of the Work and to communicate to the public those public recitations, by any means or process, including by wire or wireless means or public digital performances; to make available to the public Works in such a way that members of the public may access these Works from a place and at a place individually chosen by them; to perform the Work to the public by any means or process and the communication to the public of the performances of the Work, including by public digital performance; to broadcast and rebroadcast the Work by any means including signs, sounds or images.

(k) "Reproduce" means to make copies of the Work by any means including without limitation by sound or visual recordings and the right of fixation and reproducing fixations of the Work, including storage of a protected performance or phonogram in digital form or other electronic medium.

2. Fair Dealing Rights. Nothing in this License is intended to reduce, limit, or restrict any uses free from copyright or rights arising from limitations or exceptions that are provided for in connection with the copyright protection under copyright law or other applicable laws.
3. License Grant. Subject to the terms and conditions of this License, Licensor hereby grants You a worldwide, royalty-free, non-exclusive, perpetual (for the duration of the applicable copyright) license to exercise the rights in the Work as stated below:

   (a) to Reproduce the Work, to incorporate the Work into one or more Collections, and to Reproduce the Work as incorporated in the Collections;
   (b) to create and Reproduce Adaptations provided that any such Adaptation, including any translation in any medium, takes reasonable steps to clearly label, demarcate or otherwise identify that changes were made to the original Work. For example, a translation could be marked "The original work was translated from English to Spanish," or a modification could indicate "The original work has been modified.";
   (c) to Distribute and Publicly Perform the Work including as incorporated in Collections; and,
   (d) to Distribute and Publicly Perform Adaptations.
   (e) For the avoidance of doubt:
       i. Non-waivable Compulsory License Schemes. In those jurisdictions in which the right to collect royalties through any statutory or compulsory licensing scheme cannot be waived, the Licensor reserves the exclusive right to collect such royalties for any exercise by You of the rights granted under this License;
       ii. Waivable Compulsory License Schemes. In those jurisdictions in which the right to collect royalties through any statutory or compulsory licensing scheme can be waived, the Licensor waives the exclusive right to collect such royalties for any exercise by You of the rights granted under this License; and,
       iii. Voluntary License Schemes. The Licensor waives the right to collect royalties, whether individually or, in the event that the Licensor is a member of a collecting society that administers voluntary licensing schemes, via that society, from any exercise by You of the rights granted under this License.

   The above rights may be exercised in all media and formats whether now known or hereafter devised. The above rights include the right to make such modifications as are technically necessary to exercise the rights in other media and formats. Subject to Section 8(f), all rights not expressly granted by Licensor are hereby reserved.

4. Restrictions. The license granted in Section 3 above is expressly made subject to and limited by the following restrictions:

   (a) You may Distribute or Publicly Perform the Work only under the terms of this License. You must include a copy of, or the Uniform Resource Identifier (URI) for, this License with every copy of the Work You Distribute or Publicly Perform. You may not offer or impose any terms on the Work that restrict the terms of this License or the ability of the recipient of the Work to exercise the rights granted to that recipient under the terms of the License. You may not sublicense the Work. You must keep intact all notices that refer to this License and to the disclaimer of warranties with every copy of the Work

You Distribute or Publicly Perform. When You Distribute or Publicly Perform the Work, You may not impose any effective technological measures on the Work that restrict the ability of a recipient of the Work from You to exercise the rights granted to that recipient under the terms of the License. This Section 4(a) applies to the Work as incorporated in a Collection, but this does not require the Collection apart from the Work itself to be made subject to the terms of this License. If You create a Collection, upon notice from any Licensor You must, to the extent practicable, remove from the Collection any credit as required by Section 4(c), as requested. If You create an Adaptation, upon notice from any Licensor You must, to the extent practicable, remove from the Adaptation any credit as required by Section 4(c), as requested.

(b) You may Distribute or Publicly Perform an Adaptation only under the terms of: (i) this License; (ii) a later version of this License with the same License Elements as this License; (iii) a Creative Commons jurisdiction license (either this or a later license version) that contains the same License Elements as this License (*e.g.*, Attribution-ShareAlike 3.0 US)); (iv) a Creative Commons Compatible License. If you license the Adaptation under one of the licenses mentioned in (iv), you must comply with the terms of that license. If you license the Adaptation under the terms of any of the licenses mentioned in (i), (ii) or (iii) (the "Applicable License"), you must comply with the terms of the Applicable License generally and the following provisions: (I) You must include a copy of, or the URI for, the Applicable License with every copy of each Adaptation You Distribute or Publicly Perform; (II) You may not offer or impose any terms on the Adaptation that restrict the terms of the Applicable License or the ability of the recipient of the Adaptation to exercise the rights granted to that recipient under the terms of the Applicable License; (III) You must keep intact all notices that refer to the Applicable License and to the disclaimer of warranties with every copy of the Work as included in the Adaptation You Distribute or Publicly Perform; (IV) when You Distribute or Publicly Perform the Adaptation, You may not impose any effective technological measures on the Adaptation that restrict the ability of a recipient of the Adaptation from You to exercise the rights granted to that recipient under the terms of the Applicable License. This Section 4(b) applies to the Adaptation as incorporated in a Collection, but this does not require the Collection apart from the Adaptation itself to be made subject to the terms of the Applicable License.

(c) If You Distribute, or Publicly Perform the Work or any Adaptations or Collections, You must, unless a request has been made pursuant to Section 4(a), keep intact all copyright notices for the Work and provide, reasonable to the medium or means You are utilizing: (i) the name of the Original Author (or pseudonym, if applicable) if supplied, and/or if the Original Author and/or Licensor designate another party or parties (*e.g.*, a sponsor institute, publishing entity, journal) for attribution ("Attribution Parties") in Licensor's copyright notice, terms of service or by other reasonable means, the name of such party or parties; (ii) the title of the Work if supplied; (iii) to the extent reasonably practicable, the URI, if any, that Licensor specifies to be associated with the Work, unless such URI does not refer to the copyright notice or licensing information for the Work; and (iv) , consistent with Ssection 3(b), in the case of an Adaptation, a credit identifying the use of the Work in the Adaptation (*e.g.*, "French translation of the Work by Original Author," or "Screenplay based on original Work by Original Author"). The credit required by this Section 4(c) may be implemented in any reasonable manner; provided, however, that in the case of a Adaptation or Collection, at a minimum such credit will appear, if a credit for all contributing authors of the Adaptation or Collection appears, then as part of these credits and in a manner at least as prominent as the credits for the other contributing authors. For the avoidance of doubt, You may only use the credit required by this Section for the purpose of attribution in the manner set out above and, by exercising Your rights under this License, You may not implicitly or explicitly assert or imply any connection with, sponsorship or endorsement by the Original Author, Licensor and/or Attribution Parties, as appropriate, of You or Your use of the Work, without the separate, express prior written permission of the Original Author, Licensor and/or Attribution Parties.

(d) Except as otherwise agreed in writing by the Licensor or as may be otherwise permitted by applicable law, if You Reproduce, Distribute or Publicly Perform the Work either by itself or as part of any Adaptations or Collections, You must not distort, mutilate, modify or take other derogatory action in relation to the Work which would be prejudicial to the Original Author's honor or reputation. Licensor agrees that in those jurisdictions (*e.g.* Japan), in which any exercise of the right granted in Section 3(b) of this License (the right to make Adaptations) would be deemed to be a distortion, mutilation, modification or other derogatory action prejudicial to the Original Author's honor and reputation, the Licensor will waive or not assert, as appropriate, this Section, to the fullest extent permitted by the applicable national law, to enable You to reasonably exercise Your right under Section 3(b) of this License (right to make Adaptations) but not otherwise.

5. Representations, Warranties and Disclaimer
UNLESS OTHERWISE MUTUALLY AGREED TO BY THE PARTIES IN WRITING, LICENSOR OFFERS THE WORK AS-IS AND MAKES NO REPRESENTATIONS OR WARRANTIES OF ANY KIND CONCERNING THE WORK, EXPRESS, IMPLIED, STATUTORY OR OTHERWISE, INCLUDING, WITHOUT LIMITATION, WARRANTIES OF TITLE, MERCHANTIBILITY, FITNESS FOR A PARTICULAR PURPOSE, NONINFRINGEMENT, OR THE ABSENCE OF LATENT OR OTHER DEFECTS, ACCURACY, OR THE PRESENCE OF ABSENCE OF ERRORS, WHETHER OR NOT DISCOVERABLE. SOME JURISDICTIONS DO NOT ALLOW THE EXCLUSION OF IMPLIED WARRANTIES, SO SUCH EXCLUSION MAY NOT APPLY TO YOU.

6. Limitation on Liability. EXCEPT TO THE EXTENT REQUIRED BY APPLICABLE LAW, IN NO EVENT WILL LICENSOR BE LIABLE TO YOU ON ANY LEGAL THEORY FOR ANY SPECIAL, INCIDENTAL, CONSEQUENTIAL, PUNITIVE OR EXEMPLARY DAMAGES ARISING OUT OF THIS LICENSE OR THE USE OF THE WORK, EVEN IF LICENSOR HAS BEEN ADVISED OF THE POSSIBILITY OF SUCH DAMAGES.

7. Termination

(a) This License and the rights granted hereunder will terminate automatically upon any breach by You of the terms of this License. Individuals or entities who have received Adaptations or Collections from You under this License, however, will not have their licenses terminated provided such individuals or entities remain in full compliance with those licenses. Sections 1, 2, 5, 6, 7, and 8 will survive any termination of this License.

(b) Subject to the above terms and conditions, the license granted here is perpetual (for the duration of the applicable copyright in the Work). Notwithstanding the above, Licensor reserves the right to release the Work under different license terms or to stop distributing the Work at any time; provided, however that any such election will not serve to withdraw this License (or any other license that has been, or is required to be, granted under the terms of this License), and this License will continue in full force and effect unless terminated as stated above.

8. Miscellaneous

(a) Each time You Distribute or Publicly Perform the Work or a Collection, the Licensor offers to the recipient a license to the Work on the same terms and conditions as the license granted to You under this License.

(b) Each time You Distribute or Publicly Perform an Adaptation, Licensor offers to the recipient a license to the original Work on the same terms and conditions as the license granted to You under this License.

(c) If any provision of this License is invalid or unenforceable under applicable law, it shall not affect the validity or enforceability of the remainder of the terms of this License, and without further action by the parties to this agreement, such provision shall be reformed to the minimum extent necessary to make such provision valid and enforceable.

(d) No term or provision of this License shall be deemed waived and no breach consented to unless such waiver or consent shall be in writing and signed by the party to be charged with such waiver or consent.

(e) This License constitutes the entire agreement between the parties with respect to the Work licensed here. There are no understandings, agreements or representations with respect to the Work not specified here. Licensor shall not be bound by any additional provisions that may appear in any communication from You. This License may not be modified without the mutual written agreement of the Licensor and You.

(f) The rights granted under, and the subject matter referenced, in this License were drafted utilizing the terminology of the Berne Convention for the Protection of Literary and Artistic Works (as amended on September 28, 1979), the Rome Convention of 1961, the WIPO Copyright Treaty of 1996, the WIPO Performances and Phonograms Treaty of 1996 and the Universal Copyright Convention (as revised on July 24, 1971). These rights and subject matter take effect in the relevant jurisdiction in which the License terms are sought to be enforced according to the corresponding provisions of the implementation of those treaty provisions in the applicable national law. If the standard suite of rights granted under applicable copyright law includes additional rights not granted under this License, such additional rights are deemed to be included in the License; this License is not intended to restrict the license of any rights under applicable law.

Creative Commons Notice

Creative Commons is not a party to this License, and makes no warranty whatsoever in connection with the Work. Creative Commons will not be liable to You or any party on any legal theory for any damages whatsoever, including without limitation any general, special, incidental or consequential damages arising in connection to this license. Notwithstanding the foregoing two (2) sentences, if Creative Commons has expressly identified itself as the Licensor hereunder, it shall have all rights and obligations of Licensor.

Except for the limited purpose of indicating to the public that the Work is licensed under the CCPL, Creative Commons does not authorize the use by either party of the trademark "Creative Commons" or any related trademark or logo of Creative Commons without the prior written consent of Creative Commons. Any permitted use will be in compliance with Creative Commons' then-current trademark usage guidelines, as may be published on its website or otherwise made available upon request from time to time. For the avoidance of doubt, this trademark restriction does not form part of the License.

Creative Commons may be contacted at http://creativecommons.org/.

Glossary

Canonical Canonical, the financial backer of Ubuntu, provides support for the core Ubuntu system. It has over 500 staff members worldwide who ensure that the foundation of the operating system is stable, as well as checking all the work submitted by volunteer contributors. To learn more about Canonical, go to http://www.canonical.com.

CLI CLI or command-line interface is another name for the terminal.

cursor The (usually) blinking square or vertical line used to show you where text will appear when you start typing. You can move it around with the arrow keys on your keyboard prompt in a terminal or other text-input application.

desktop environment A generic term to describe a GUI interface for humans to interact with computers. There are many desktop environments such as GNOME, KDE, XFCE and LXDE, to name a few.

DHCP DHCP stands for *Dynamic Host Configuration Protocol*, it is used by a DHCP server to assign computers on a network an IP address automatically.

dialup connection A dialup connection is when your computer uses a modem to connect to an ISP through your telephone line.

distribution A distribution is a collection of software that is already compiled and configured ready to be installed. Ubuntu is an example of a distribution.

dual-booting Dual-booting is the process of being able to choose one of two different operating systems currently installed on a computer from the boot menu. Once selected, your computer will boot into whichever operating system you chose at the boot menu. The term dual-booting is often used generically, and may refer to booting among more than two operating systems.

encryption Encryption is a security measure, it prevents others from accessing and viewing the contents of your files and/or hard drives, the files must first be decrypted with your password.

Ethernet port An Ethernet port is what an Ethernet cable is plugged into when you are using a wired connection.

GUI The GUI (which stands for Graphical User Interface) is a type of user interface that allows humans to interact with the computer using graphics and images rather than just text.

ISP ISP stands for *Internet Service Provider*, an ISP is a company that provides you with your Internet connection.

kernel A kernel is the central portion of a Unix-based operating system, responsible for running applications, processes, and providing security for the core components.

maximize When you maximize an application in Ubuntu it will fill the whole desktop, excluding the panels.

minimize When you minimize an open application, the window will no longer be shown. If you click on a minimized application's icon in the Launcher, it will be restored to its normal state and allow you to interact with it.

output The output of a command is any text it displays on the next line after typing a command and pressing enter, *e.g.*, if you type `pwd` into a terminal and press Enter, the directory name it displays on the next line is the output.

package Packages contain software in a ready-to-install format. Most of the time you can use the Software Center instead of manually installing packages. Packages have a .deb extension in Ubuntu.

parameter Parameters are special options that you can use with other commands in the terminal to make that command behave differently, this can make a lot of commands far more useful.

partition A partition is an area of allocated space on a hard drive where you can put data.

partitioning partitioning is the process of creating a partition.

prompt The prompt displays some useful information about your computer. It can be customized to display in different colors, display the time, date, and current directory or almost anything else you like.

proprietary Software made by companies that don't release their source code under an open source license.

router A router is a specially designed computer that, using its software and hardware, routes information from the Internet to a network. It is also sometimes called a gateway.

server A server is a computer that runs a specialized operating system and provides services to computers that connect to it and make a request.

shell The terminal gives access to the shell, when you type a command into the terminal and press enter the shell takes that command and performs the relevant action.

Software Center The Software Center is where you can easily manage software installation and removal as well as the ability to manage software installed via Personal Package Archives.

terminal The terminal is Ubuntu's text-based interface. It is a method of controlling the operating system using only commands entered via the keyboard as opposed to using a GUI like Unity.

USB Universal Serial Bus is a standard interface specification for connecting peripheral hardware devices to computers. USB devices range from external hard drives to scanners and printers.

wired connection A wired connection is when your computer is physically connected to a router or Ethernet port with a cable. This is the most common method of connecting to the Internet and local network for desktop computers.

wireless connection A network connection that uses a wireless signal to communicate with either a router, access point, or computer.

Credits

This manual wouldn't have been possible without the efforts and contributions from the following people:

Team leads

Kevin Godby—Lead TeXnician
John Xygonakis—Authors Coordinator & Translation Maintainer
Hannie Dumoleyn—Editors Coordinator & Translation Maintainer
Thorsten Wilms—Design
Adnane Belmadiaf—Web development

Authors

Mario Burgos	Sayantan Das	Andrew Montag
John Cave	Patrick Dickey	Tony Pursell
Jim Connett	Herat Gandhi Amrish	Mike Romard

Editors

Mario Burgos	Carsten Gerlach	Tony Pursell
Jim Connett	Kevin Godby	
Hannie Dumoleyn	Paddy Landau	

Screenshots

Patrick Dickey   Carsten Gerlach

Designers

Thorsten Wilms

Developers

Adnane Belmadiaf   Kevin Godby

Translation editors

Fran Diéguez (Galician)	Xuacu Saturio (Asturian)	Chris Woollard (British English)
Hannie Dumoleyn (Dutch)	Daniel Schury (German)	John Xygonakis (Greek)
Shazedur Rahim Joardar (Bengali)	Shrinivasan (Tamil)	

Past contributors

Bryan Behrenshausen (Author)	Will Kromer (Author)
Senthil Velan Bhooplan (Author)	Simon Lewis (Author)
Che Dean (Author)	Ryan Macnish (Author)
Rick Fosburgh (Editor-in-Chief)	Mez Pahlan (Author)
Benjamin Humphrey (Project Founder)	Vibhav Pant (Editor)

Brian Peredo (Author)
Joel Pickett (Author)
Kev Quirk (Author)
Kartik Sulakhe (Author)

Tom Swartz (Author)
David Wales (Author)
Chris Woollard (Editor)

Index

32-bit versus 64-bit, 9–10

accessibility, 32
   screen reader, 32
Apple, *see* MacBook
applications
   adding and removing, 24
   presentation, *see* LibreOffice
   running, 23
   searching, 25
   spreadsheet, *see* LibreOffice
   word processor, *see* LibreOffice
audio, *see* sound *and* music
audio, playing, *see* Rhythmbox

Bluetooth, 95
booting
   troubleshooting, 115

camera, importing photos, 67
Canonical, 6
CDs and DVDs
   blanking, 76
   burning, 75–78
   codecs, 70
   copying, 77
   playing, 70, 71
   ripping, 71
cloud storage, *see* Ubuntu One
codecs
   audio, 74
   video, 70
command line, *see* terminal

Dash, 24
Debian, 6, *see also* Linux
desktop
   background, 22
   customization, 31
      appearance, 31
      background, 32
      theme, 31
   go, 28
   menu bar, 22
   sharing, 62
disk, *see* CDs and DVDs
display
   adding secondary, 90–91
   changing resolution, 90
   troubleshooting, 118
drivers, 89–90
dual-booting, 13
DVDs and CDs, *see* CDs and DVDs

EeePC
   troubleshooting, 119
email, *see* Thunderbird
Empathy, 59–63
   add accounts, 59
   chatting, 60–61
   desktop sharing, 62
   setup, 59
encryption, *see* security

Facebook, *see* Gwibber
file system structure, 108–109
files
   browsing, 28
   Nautilus
      opening files, 29
   recovering, 117
   sync, *see* Ubuntu One
files and folders
   copying, 30
   creating, 29
   displaying hidden, 29
   moving, 30
   searching, 30–31
Firefox, 46–54
Firewall
   using, 113
firewall
   installing, 113
FireWire, *see* IEEE 1394

groups, *see also* users
   adding, 112
   deleting, 112
   files and folders, 113
   managing, 112
   modifying, 112
Gwibber, 63–66

hardware
   troubleshooting, 120
help
   Ask Ubuntu, 125
   documentation, 124
   forums, 124
   Full Circle Magazine, 125
   general help, 34
   heads-up display (HUD), 34
   Launchpad Answers, 124
   live chat, 124
   online, 34
home folder, 28

IEEE 1394, 94
installing Ubuntu in Windows, 18–19
instant messaging, *see* Empathy
Internet
   browsing, 46–54
   connecting, 40–46
   wireless, 42
Internet radio, 72

kernel, 6

Launcher, 23
   running applications, 23
LibreOffice, 78
Linux, 6–7
Linux distributions, 121–122
Live DVD, *see* Ubuntu Live DVD
locking the screen, 34
logging out, 33
login options, 16

Mac OS X, *see* MacBook
MacBook
   troubleshooting, 119
microblogging, *see* Gwibber
monitor, *see* display
mounting devices, 110
Movie Player, 69
music, *see* Rhythmbox
   downloading, 74

Nautilus, 28
   multiple tabs, 30
   multiple windows, 30
   navigating, 29
   window, 28
NetworkManager, 40

open-source software, 121

password, *see* security
photos, *see also* Shotwell
   editing, 68
   importing, 67
   viewing, 66
podcasts, 72
presentation application, 78
printer, 91
   add via USB, 91
   adding via network, 91

rebooting, 33
Rhythmbox, 70–75

Internet radio, 72
playing music, 71
podcasts, 72

scanner, 93
　troubleshooting, 94
screen, *see* display
security
　encryption, 114
　introduction, 110
　passwords, 111
　permissions, 110
　resetting passwords, 116
　screen locking, 111
　system updates, 113
Shotwell, 66–69
shutting down, 33
Shuttleworth, Mark, 6
slide show, *see* LibreOffice
software
　adding repository, 103–104
　email, 37
　finding applications, 98
　installation history, 101
　installing, 98–100
　managing, 101
　manual installation, 104–105
　movie players, 38
　multimedia players, 38
　music players, 38
　office suites, 37
　podcast readers, 38
　presentation, 37
　recommendations, 101
　removing, 100
　repositories, 102
　servers, 103
　spreadsheet, 37

video players, 38
web browser, 37
word processor, 37
Software Center, 97
sound
　input, 93
　output, 92
　recording, 93
　troubleshooting, 118
　volume, 92
sound effects, 93
spreadsheet, 78
start up, *see* boot
suspending the computer, 33
system requirements, 9

terminal
　about, 107
　using, 108
Thunderbird, 55–59
　setup, 55
torrent
　Ubuntu image, 10
Twitter, *see* Gwibber

Ubuntu
　alternate interfaces, 122–123
　bootable USB drive, 10
　definition of, 5
　derivatives, 122
　downloading, 9
　Edubuntu, 123
　history of, 6
　installing, 11–17
　Mythbuntu, 123
　philosophy of, 5
　Server Edition, 123
　Ubuntu Studio, 123
Ubuntu Live DVD, 10–11

Ubuntu One, 78–87
Ubuntu Promise, 6
Ubuntu Software Center, 97
Unity, 21
Unix, 6, 7
unmounting devices, 110
updates
　about, 105–106
　automatic, 106
　release updates, 106
USB, 94
users, *see also* groups
　adding, 112
　creating during installation, 15–16
　deleting, 112
　managing, 111
　modifying, 112

video
　troubleshooting, 118
videos
　codecs, 70
　playing, 69
volume, *see* sound

webcam, 93
Wi-Fi, 42
windows, 26
　closing, 26
　force on top, 27
　minimizing, 26
　moving, 27
　moving between, 27
　resizing, 27
　restoring, 26
　switching, 27
word processor, 78
workspaces, 26

COLOPHON

This book was typeset with X⅃ᴇLᴀTᴇX.

The book design is based on the Tufte-LaTeX document classes available at http://code.google.com/p/tufte-latex/.

The text face is Linux Libertine, designed by Philipp H. Poll. It is an open font available at http://linuxlibertine.sf.net/.

The captions and margin notes are set in Ubuntu, a font commissioned by Canonical and designed by Dalton Maag. It is freely available for download at http://font.ubuntu.com/.

The terminal text and keystrokes are set in DejaVu Sans Mono (available at http://dejavu-fonts.org/), originally developed by Bitstream, Inc. as Bitstream Vera.

The cover and title page pictograms contain shapes taken from the Humanity icon set, available at https://launchpad.net/humanity.

The title page and cover were designed using Inkscape, available at http://inkscape.org/.

Printed in Great Britain
by Amazon.co.uk, Ltd.,
Marston Gate.